Survival 101

Gordon Jackson

DR Publishers
Bon Air, Virginia

Copyright and Ordering

Copyright © 2015 Gordon D Jackson.

All rights reserved.

Printed in the United States of America.
Typographical corrections were incorporated in March 2016.

Ordering Information

Please visit drpublishers.com to find: (1) Links to sites which accept online orders, (2) E-Book availability, and (3) Information on ordering multipacks, which provide significant savings for those who want to share this book with others.

ISBN Numbers

ISBN 10: 0-9963941-3-0-9

ISBN 13: 978-0-9963941-0-9

Military Edition

This book is the Military Edition of ISBN 978-0-9963941-3-0: "Silver Linings: Overcoming with Optimism - A Memoir" by the same author.

Contact Information

DR Publishers

PO Box 35171

Bon Air, Virginia 23235

www.drpublishers.com

Dedication

To Anne, without whom the creativity inside me might never have been released.

Acknowledgments

General

I am grateful that our family was able to find many sources of encouragement, which raised our level of optimism to traverse difficulties and not give up. In particular, Denis and Bill have been two stalwart friends, who have never shrunk back from the provision of palpable assistance during some of our darkest hours.

Creative Editor

My wife, Cindy, deserves her own *Medal of Honor* for her steadfast encouragement throughout this long writing assignment and for her tireless provision of welcomed and insightful creative editorial feedback.

Strategic Coach

Through Anne, my path crossed with that of a business professor, who provided a listening ear and shared his honest perceptive observations that have helped me to uncover a path for my return to the academic world and my entry into the world of creative writing.

Photographs & Images

Flickr. Creative Commons 2.0 License (Chapters 11, 15, 17, 18, 19)
Hirkimer, Sir. Express written permission. (Chapters 2, 16)
Jackson, Gordon (Chapters 1, 6, 12, 14, 20)
Lambert Sr., William (Chapter 21)
Library of Congress (Chapters 3, 4, 5, 7, 8, 9, 10)
Wikipedia. Creative Commons Attribution-Share Alike 2.5
    Generic license. (Chapter 13)

Table of Contents

1. Storytelling 1
   Triangle, VA – London, England

2. The Other Side of the Tracks 5
   Battersea, London

3. We Shall Fight in the Streets 9
   London

4. Family Identity 13
   London

5. Medicating Pain 17
   Tokyo – Hong Kong – London - Gillingham, Kent

6. Keep Calm and Carry On 21
   London – Bound Brook, NJ

7. Baby It's Cold Outside 25
   Buffalo, NY

8. All Wet 29
   Tonawanda, NY – Northern Michigan

9. Steal My Purse 33
   Piccadilly Circus, London – Southwark, London

10. On a Wing and a Prayer 37
    Los Angeles, CA – Toronto, Canada

11. A Sticky Wicket 41
    London – Buffalo, NY

12. **Anne** 45
   Nyack, NY

13. **Love Is All You Need** 49
   Buffalo, NY – Puerto Rico – The Dominican Republic

14. **Showing Up** 53
   Philadelphia, PA

15. **Stepping Stones** 57
   London – Buffalo, NY – Richmond, VA

16. **A Track to Run On** 61
   London – Buffalo, NY – Richmond, VA

17. **Junk or Treasure?** 65
   Buffalo, NY

18. **On Her Majesty's Secret Service** 69
   London – Niagara Falls – Buffalo NY

19. **Tackle Low – Tackle Hard – Fearlessly** 73
   London – Germany – Buffalo, NY

20. **Rome – The Eternal City** 77
   Rome, Italy

21. **Stand by Me** 81
   Neath, Wales & Kyushu, Japan – London – Tokyo
   Hong Kong – London - Gillingham, Kent

   References 85

   Index 87

1. Storytelling

National Museum of the Marine Corps – Triangle VA (Jackson)

I entered the spacious lobby of the National Museum of the US Marine Corps and Sargent Major Lonnie Martin warmly welcomed me to his tour group, where he enthusiastically narrated fascinating stories about his extraordinary service mostly spent on the front lines. One particular narrative about pirates cemented my understanding of how storytelling is used to develop the warrior mindset so that Marines can improvise, adapt and overcome the enemy.

Lonnie said that a while ago when piracy was uncommon, a small section of a Marine Expeditionary Unit was deployed to assault and occupy a vessel held by enemy combatants. When the officer-in-charge was given the assault objective, a story popped into his mind. He recalled that during a conversation held over drinks, he had heard about the tactics that Marines had used to successfully breach, occupy, and clear buildings of enemy combatants. Their tactical advantage came from entering via the roof and then moving down to lower floors because it provided an element of surprise and offered better vantage points to view locations of hidden threats.

Although the ship was not a fixed object, the officer wondered if a similar tactical advantage could be gained in his present situation. With limited time to take action and no time to perform reconnaissance, he decided to leverage what he had learned from listening to a story.

The assaulting force breached the ship at its bridge and was able to occupy and clear the ship from top to bottom. Remembering the war story, the officer benefited from the understanding that those images triggered in his mind.

Through his description of what happened, Lonnie demonstrated how the Marines retell stories to increase force readiness. Educators call this narrative pedagogy, which is the use of storytelling as a way to deliver a memorable learning experience. Storytelling helps us use our imagination and develop critical thinking skills. In so doing, we will better understand the significance of the experiences. Then we will receive the benefit of being able to recall and apply this knowledge in the future (Woodhouse).

Although our tour was only slated to last one hour, we found ourselves so immersed in the Marine experience that we willingly kept listening well-beyond the scheduled ending time for our visit.

After I left the museum, I recalled how my class of undergraduate chemical engineers learned from sad but true stories delivered in a humorous style by Mr. O'Reilly, an

Inspector from HM Factory Inspectorate (US: Occupational Safety and Health Administration - OSHA).

Mr. O'Reilly was a riveting speaker who used humorous insight when sharing the principles of industrial safety in chemical plants. We laughed frequently, even though the real life situations he described were incredibly sad:

> There was a situation at a sugar refinery, when one worker collapsed as he cleaned up residual sludge, inside an open tank. The second worker at the edge of the tank impulsively rushed in to help his mate, but also collapsed. A third followed suite. Only the fourth person saw the gravity of the situation and obtained breathing gear before trying to help the others. The previous three workers sadly perished.

For decades, I continued using the principles that are encapsulated in his case study. Recently, I was faced with a time-sensitive mold removal project needed to complete the sale of our home; I remembered those sugar refinery workers. I asked myself three questions. Am I compctent to complete the job safely? If so, do I have the required protective gear? What is the best way to proceed?

A professor from my Alma Mater was often called upon to chair public inquiries into major chemical plant disasters. He taught a course about industrial safety, and was also a firm believer that the best way to impact someone for life, was to tell plenty of vivid stories. Wouldn't you know it? He was in the same classroom where we were both engaged by Mr. O'Reilly's delivery style. Fancy that.

Following in the steps of my professor friend, I recounted past events in order to make computer security concepts memorable. For example, students perked up their ears whenever I talked about the impact of the 9-11 terrorist attack on data integrity and availability.

The US Marines, industrial safety experts, and the teachers in this chapter have all utilized historical narratives to equip their listeners to better deal with difficult circumstances they currently face or might face at some future time.

The images associated with a story are usually more readily recalled than the facts. Those images can help unleash inspiration to handle the issue at hand and may also release useful information from the recesses of the brain. In addition to being useful, a well-told story can entertain.

A friend read one of these chapters and came up to me with a big smile and said, "You just had to put your head out of the steam train window, after your mother told you not to." I just smiled, and said, "That's just the way I am – looking for the next adventure."

I invite you to join me on a trip back through time, experience different cultures and visit different places and countries. This journey may cause laughter or may trigger an unanticipated emotion. In the end, I hope that the short stories will enrich your life and also provide you with some practical insights and understanding that will help you survive and rise above the stresses of daily life.

2. The Other Side of the Tracks

Stewarts Lane – Battersea, London (Hirkimer, 1963)

A part of a town that is considered poor and dangerous
(Cambridge University Press)

I recently read that the idiom to live on the other side of the tracks hearkened back to the days of steam engines. The soot and smoke from the engines and the direction of the prevailing winds relative to the location of the tracks made some parts of town more desirable than others. Our first family home was on Lockington Road, which nestled in the shadows of Battersea Power Station, the gas works and the Battersea Dogs Home.

Within a stone's throw of our humble abode, on our side of the tracks, I could admire the Decca Radio and TV building (Left-hand side in the picture above). Decca built the state-of-the-art line of Stereo Decola Separates. The design appealed to the ladies and the performance specifications to the gentlemen

("Audio"). These products catered to the requirements of those who lived on the better side of the tracks.

Growing up, my Mum repeatedly told me that I should never disclose the location of where we lived. She was probably ashamed of where we found ourselves. This was not by choice, but by the chain of events that culminated in my parents' return to England. They were destitute and had a young child in tow.

My Mum told me that our first furniture was comprised of several designer orange crates. Once a week, our budget included a modicum of meat. My parents relied on rent control tribunals to reduce our expenses to an affordable level and to legally ensure that we could not be evicted for six months. My Mum said, "One landlord was so annoyed that he tried to force us to leave by spreading smelly things nearby. An exception was a kind Jewish landlord who did not retaliate, but showed pity." Looking back, I wonder if he had been impacted by the Holocaust. Perhaps he had decided to eschew justifiable bitterness and show compassion instead.

Regardless of how others viewed our humble abode, it was home. There were many memorable, difficult and dangerous highlights, but for our family, it was still home. It was similar to the fulfillment of Eliza Doolittle's dream in *My Fair Lady*:

> All I want is a room somewhere
> Far away from the cold night air
> With one enormous chair
> Oh, wouldn't it be loverly? (Lerner)

When in 1964, my Dad took me to the opening season of *My Fair Lady* in Leicester Square; I was captivated by those words of Eliza Doolittle. Perhaps it was because I subconsciously related to the sentiment expressed in the musical.

Over time, geographical locations change and so do we. The rough working-class neighborhood of Battersea has now become gentrified. We used to walk every week to the Nine Elms Public Baths. Now, Nine Elms is the location of the construction site for the new US Embassy in London. Therefore, there is now no longer any need to use furtive tones about the location of where I grew up. Shortly, I will be able to be bold and accurate when I say, "I grew up within walking distance of the American Embassy."

Back then, racial slurs and name-calling were a part of my experience in the neighborhood. Even though societal discrimination was pervasive, I would travel alone to central London. My Mum taught me how to avoid interaction with kids who seemed antagonistic. Every day, I caught the Southern Region train from Battersea Park to Victoria Station. Then I walked half a mile up Victoria Street to Mrs. Ingham's Kindergarten near the Strutton Ground market. On my return, I would sometimes stop and buy a bunch of violets for my Mum. More often than not, I would buy one bunch, and the street vendor would give me several more. Such a small gift inevitably cheered up my Mum who continually sacrificed for my well-being.

While my Dad worked for HM Customs and Excise at Hayes Wharf in London, he started a home-based scientific and technical Japanese to English translation service. This business grew to the point that he quit his day job, and my Mum worked beside him.

Each week he visited HK Lewis's private technical lending library on Gower Street and borrowed books to complete his translation work accurately. Books were his friends and afforded him the education he was denied in Japan because of his family's pro-West stance in the 1930's. They sent him to an American Missionary School where he learned English. However, he could not then attend an Imperial University. Even without a formal education, he was honored to represent the Association for Information Management on the British Standards committee for the Romanization of Japanese.

My parents' entrepreneurial venture would ultimately enable us to make annual pilgrimages to Europe. I can vividly remember times when I sat with my parents in Rome at street-side café tables drinking a Coke. This was so different from the daily humdrum and challenging life we experienced in Battersea.

It is inspiring to contrast how my parents arrived in London with nothing but ended their lives helping the next generation to buy their first home and bring up their grand-children.

My parents demonstrated that it was possible to start on the wrong side of the tracks but finish in a completely different place and situation. Such a transformation required endurance and sacrifice. Undoubtedly, they had both been inspired by the words of Winston Churchill:

> Never give in, never give in, never, never, never-in nothing great or small, large or petty, never give in except to convictions of honour and good sense.
> (Churchill, "Never Give In")

3. We Shall Fight in the Streets

London is still "taking it" (International News)

It's impossible to know what helped shape our family resolve to persevere through the difficulties that life presented. My Dad had a keen sense of the importance of being true to his ideology. A conversation with my Mum revealed the required mindset to survive Hitler's bombs that exploded on nearby streets.

Apart from heredity, perhaps my personal inspiration came from my parents' lives and a life-long admiration of Sir Winston Churchill, whom Londoners affectionately called *Winnie*. Although I did not have to live through Hitler's Blitz, years later, I was a bomb warden during the IRA terrorist bombings of London.

In all our lives, we accepted and paid due homage to the inspiration of Britain's fearless leader, at a time when victory seemed far from certain:

> We shall go on to the end, we shall fight in France, we shall fight on the seas and oceans, we shall fight with growing confidence and growing strength in the air, we shall defend our Island, whatever the cost may be, we shall fight on the beaches, we shall fight on the landing grounds, we shall fight in the fields and in the streets, we shall fight in the hills; we shall never surrender. (Churchill, "We Shall Fight")

As a young teenager, I asked Mum, "How did you ever survive the Blitz?" With her Welsh lilt, she said:

> The Nazi buzz bombs made a sound like a motorcycle in the sky. Then the engine stopped and you knew that the bomb was coming down. One night, I counted forty-three bombs. Another night I heard a sound like someone scratched the tile roof with a knife. Then I heard a loud bang and the house shook. That bomb landed a couple of streets over. If you couldn't get to sleep, you could call the telephone operator. They would listen, and this helped to pull yourself together. You had to go about your business. You had to accept that if your name was written on the bomb, it would find you.

I listened to my Mum in awe, not realizing that my time to survive exploding bombs on London streets was yet to come.

The 31st of October 1971 was the date when a bomb exploded on the 33rd floor of the Post Office Tower in London. It marked the beginning of the Irish Republican Army's (IRA) bombing blitz of central London:

The IRA seemed to dominate the news throughout the 70's. ... On February the 22nd 1973, the IRA killed seven civilians in the Aldershot bombing. In that same year a car bomb exploded outside the Old Bailey in London and on September the 10th the IRA detonated bombs in Kings Cross Station and Euston Station. ... The Houses of Parliament were targeted ... (Mc Hough)

At this time, I was wrapping up my undergraduate studies at Imperial College. During my postgraduate years, Londoners once again developed standard operating procedures to become more vigilant and deal with the many bombs. Once again, we were not going to give in to terrorism. At college, I was an appointed Bomb Warden, who would be called upon periodically to check neighboring laboratories for suspicious packages.

After moving to America, I was still emotionally impacted by on-going terrorism in London. When I heard of the 1982 Hyde Park bombing of the Household Cavalry, I thought of my previously peaceful park walks in the same area. When, in 1983, Harrods was bombed, I remembered shopping for delicious French Gateaux at the store that was close to my student residence. In 1991, on a visit to England shortly after the rush-hour bombing of Victoria Station, I was transfixed by the stain of blood on the station concourse: a stark and tangible reminder of the violent, unrelenting adversity faced by Londoners who resolutely and staunchly refused to give in.

Looking back, it is evident that Sir Winston Churchill's leadership had helped many Londoners survive. Because of my admiration for what he had done, I experienced a loss when he died in 1965. Even as a teenager, I felt compelled to be one of the band of mourners who slowly and contemplatively filed past the cataflague upon which the coffin of my hero rested. Independent Television News (ITN) sets the stage for this moment in history:

> In a moving display of homage, thousands of mourners will today (Wednesday) file past the coffin of Sir Winston Churchill lying-in-state in the historic Westminster Hall, at the Houses of Parliament. At nine o'clock this morning the three day period of lying-in-state began with Mr. Harold Wilson, the Prime Minister, and his wife being the first to pay their last respects.
>
> Mourners waited throughout a frosty night for admittance to the "Hall of Kings". Most of the hardy band had waited since yesterday afternoon to be among the first to pay homage to the departed statesman. But before the public were allowed in members of both houses of parliament, the Royal Household and the staff of the Palace of Westminster moved in procession past the bier. (Reuters)

As I slowly walked over the great stone floor of Westminster Hall's imposing gothic structure, the sound of my footsteps was muffled by the judicious placement of carpet. The poignancy of this solemn moment was inescapable.

Mum's life had inspired me. Winston Churchill had inspired her. Now our hero was no more.

4. Family Identity

Relocation Center – Manzanar, California (Adams)

The image of the Japanese Internment Camp above is a stark reminder of how the United States reacted in time of war to a perceived threat. Sadly, this impacted Japanese Americans who had emigrated from Japan to escape from the rising reach of the Japanese military. This triggered in them the release of exceptionally intense feelings of betrayal and isolation.

Although those who were interned might not have been privy to the inspiring words of Winston Churchill, they never gave up. They tirelessly worked to maintain their family identity in the midst of the heartache which has only recently been voiced publicly.

The work of one organization, which provides ways to tell the story of the effect of WW II on Japanese Americans and their offspring, impacted me in a very surprising way. A visit to the Japanese American National Museum in Los Angeles gave me a profound understanding of the intensity of my parent's unspoken feelings.

As I approached a section of a World War II billet, I discovered that it was previously a part of an Internment Camp. Being naturally inquisitive, I wanted to know the story behind this gaunt reminder of the past. I read that a number of children of first generation Japanese immigrant parents had decided to be a part of the Museum's project to create a core exhibit. They visited an actual camp, took apart a billet and reassembled the pieces to provide an exhibit that was a visually effective reminder of the past.

Those who participated were asked to contribute their oral history through written diary entries that articulated their thoughts and feelings as they completed their mission. This initial work has been subsequently extended through the Museum's on-line remembrance-project.org website.

One particular diary entry caused me to cry because it abruptly removed the veil that previously blocked my understanding of the pain that my parents had felt:

> During this project, I finally understood the depth of the pain my parents had experienced, but had never been able to express. (Jackson, Personal Diary, April 18, 2007)

My Dad's wartime experience was very different from those who were interned, but the intensity of feelings triggered by the war was undoubtedly similar, albeit in a different country.

My Dad was not interned during World War II because he worked for the British Foreign Office in political and military intelligence. He also provided wartime radio broadcasting in

Japanese. His broadcasts were a part of the allied forces' antidote to Tokyo Rose's wartime radio propaganda. The allied forces broadcast to Japanese soldiers in Japanese. This distinguished wartime service resulted in his being granted British Citizenship. Shortly before the war ended, Dad was reassigned to the Japanese Language section of the BBC World Service in Bush House, London. After the war, Scotland Yard's Special Branch reviewed his application for citizenship, which was granted.

In London, his desire to have a family, maintain his family identity and have a child came closer to reality. There he met his life-long companion, my Mum.

Like many of my Dad's generation and ethnic origin, he was proud of his family lineage. He was born in Kyushu, Japan to a family of Samurai descent. Because his original family name, Nakano, differs from mine, Jackson, many have asked, "Why is your last name Jackson?"

Until a couple of years ago, I did not know the answer to that question. In December 2012, I finally decided to read some of the paperwork my Dad had kept concerning his service during the Second World War. This triggered visits to the UK National Archives in Kew Gardens, London and the US National Archives in College Park, MD. The fascinating findings from this research will be the basis for another book.

Because of archival and other research, I now know why my last name is Jackson, but my Dad's was Nakano.

It turns out that the name change became official on the dock in Singapore, where a British Passport Control Officer gave my Dad legal paperwork that established his new identity. My Dad's boss at the British Foreign Office's

Far Eastern Bureau in Shanghai, China, had told him that he would only be permitted to choose his first name. His boss would chose his new last name for reasons that became apparent during the historical research I performed.

A name change was necessitated by the fact that the Japanese military distrusted my Dad. Later, Scotland Yard's Special Branch would report that the Foreign Office had reason to believe that there was an order out for my Dad's apprehension and execution.

After the War, my parents were rejected by much of society because many English families had been impacted by the atrocities committed by the Japanese military. Many had heard sad stories from prisoners of war. Few knew that my Dad had served honorably as a part of the Allied Forces intelligence community.

My Dad had stayed true to his Samurai lineage. At any time, he was willing to die for his core beliefs. His family believed that the militaristic rise in Japan was unbecoming to the democratic process. Therefore, they fully supported my Dad's wartime pursuits.

Although my Dad's name was changed, not even World War II could eliminate his family identity.

Despite rejection and isolation, my Dad stayed the course and faithfully maintained his family's honor and identity, which now continues for two more generations.

5. Medicating Pain

Sake Cup (Utamaro)

We found out soon enough that whatever we were drinking,
snorting, smoking, buying, debting, eating, loving or
having sex with was our medication to hide pain. (Wholey)

When I ponder the impact of war on my parents, I
have come to believe that for most of their lives they suffered
post-traumatic stress. Their feelings of alienation from the
British society my Dad had helped to protect engendered deep
emotional pain. For most of their lives, smoking and drinking
provided a modicum of relief.

Although I was an adult child of functioning alcoholic parents, their drinking never resulted in physical abuse or lack of financial provision within their sometimes limited means.

My Dad had been denied a college education in Japan because of his family's decision to align themselves with Western Democratic ideology. Therefore, my parents wanted me to have the best education possible. Their desires became reality. They enrolled me at Highfield School to prepare me for the Emanuel School entrance examinations. Emanuel prepared me for university. My Dad had an extremely high opinion of Imperial College of Science Technology and Medicine near Kensington Palace – the residence of former Princess Diana. The undergraduate degree I obtained from Imperial was in chemical engineering. I was then afforded the wonderful opportunity to stay on and complete a PhD in computer applications applied to chemical plant design. I thoroughly enjoyed the seven years at college in this exceptionally ritzy part of London. It was a stark contrast to my earlier life living on the other side of the tracks in Battersea.

Studying was win-win. Both my parents felt that a good education would help me surmount the obstacles that society might present to my career development. Reading books and studying was thoroughly enjoyable. Learning was always satisfying but difficult – I just had to slog through. Perhaps because of the extensive technical library my father assembled for this scientific and technical Japanese to English translation business, I have always had a deep love of books. Maybe this is hereditary because my oldest daughter is a librarian.

To relax from my studies, I would often listen to the radio. I particularly related to a popular Paul Simon song of the sixties:

> A winter's day
> In a deep and dark December;
> I am alone,
> Gazing from my window to the streets below
> On a freshly fallen silent shroud of snow.
> I am a rock; I am an island.
> I've built walls,
> A fortress deep and mighty,
> That none may penetrate.
> I have no need of friendship;
> Friendship causes pain.
> It's laughter and it's loving I disdain.
> …
> I have my books
> And my poetry to protect me;
> I am shielded in my armor,
> Hiding in my room, safe within my womb.
> I touch no one and no one touches me.
> And a rock feels no pain;
> And an island never cries. (Simon)

Later, I realized that the words were a self-portrait. Studying provided a way of escape. I had shut down emotionally. This course of action unwittingly and unintentionally caused my parents to suffer more pain as they felt rejected by the son for whom they had made many sacrifices.

By the time I went to university, my parents' financial situation had improved dramatically. This had required a dedication that necessitated that they worked in their business seven days a week.

Despite having an excellent education, I had no answer to the question my Mum would ask me frequently as I was growing up, "What is the point of living?" I would always respond, "There is one." Then she would ask, "What is it?" I remained silent, not knowing the answer.

In college, I continued studying diligently. However, I would drink regularly and limit the amount of time for trips back home. It was too difficult to spend extended periods at home because I had not yet been able to uncork the bottle which contained a whole gamut of emotions and understandings.

My parents were delighted that my studies led to the opportunity to move to the USA. Union Carbide recruited me in London to work in their Tonawanda, NY research facility.

Physical separation brought fresh perspectives and healing. Ultimately, both my Mum and my Dad found freedom.

It took me a long time to realize, accept and understand the extent to which the past had boxed Mum and Dad into emotional prisons. Their form of pain medication was a completely natural response. I only had power to change myself and to become a more caring son. In their twilight years, they received a wonderful new zest for living. Once again, we could function as a loving family that certainly had battle scars but were no longer separated by the consequences of war.

6. Keep Calm and Carry On

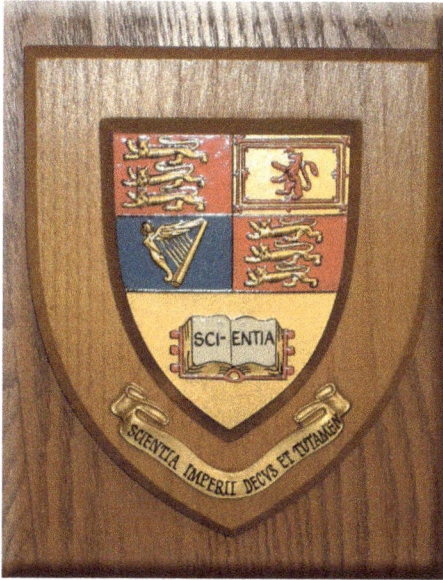

Imperial College Crest – London (Jackson)

During wartime, survival and victory were partly achieved through the manifestation of an English characteristic to maintain rationality and composure regardless of the circumstances. To successfully navigate my US job interview required me to appear imperturbable, when in reality I was just learning how to fly by the seat of my pants (Carrigan). On my first trip across the big pond, I was mistakenly lulled into a false sense of security by believing the words and sentiment aptly expressed by Oscar Wilde:

> We have really everything in common with America nowadays, except, of course, language. (Mason)

With that same sense of adventure that I had experienced on family trips to Europe, I excitedly boarded the British Airways plane at Heathrow Airport. Union Carbide

Corporation had invited me to visit their Chemicals and Plastics division in Bound Brook, New Jersey and their Linde Industrial Gas division in Tonawanda, New York. They had suggested that I take the helicopter between JFK and Newark Airports. Then they recommended that I either caught a taxi, or rented a car to drive the thirty miles between Newark and the Travelodge Motel. Both options were problematic.

In England, I drove a car rarely. The thought of picking up a vehicle at the airport and driving to a destination on the wrong side of the road was too daunting to be entertained. On the other hand, the thought of taking a taxi for a thirty-mile trip in a foreign and unknown land seemed to offer the real possibility that I would literally be taken for a ride. While I was confident that Union Carbide would reimburse me for the fare even if it was exorbitant, I wanted to avoid embarrassment. Such a debacle would inevitably convey the wrong message about my competence. Of these two choices, taking a taxi eliminated the potential trauma of driving.

The tactic I would use as I picked up the taxi had not yet been decided. During the flight over the Atlantic I had time to think and consider the best tactical approach. It occurred to me that the taxi driver needed to think that I really knew where I wanted to go. I was already armed with driving directions for the rental car option. The way to proceed was clear, I had to memorize the directions, stay calm and appear knowledgeable. The tactic worked perfectly.

Armed with memorized driving directions, I strutted towards the taxi rank. The first driver asked in a gruff way, "Where to?" To the Travelodge Motel in Bound Brook," I said. "Where's that?" asked the driver. "Take the New Jersey

Turnpike south to exit 10. The hotel is about a mile-and-a-half away from the exit," I said portraying confidence that came from memorization.

The taxi driver obligingly told me, "Because of the distance, the fare is based on the book charge of $28." He then showed me the fare in his book.

I chose to sit next to the driver, and we had a pleasant conversation. At one point he said, "You're not from around these parts, are you?" I said, "No, I'm from London." Perhaps my response was spoken indignantly. How could he not have picked up on my accent?

In reality, I was fresh off the boat but had navigated the first challenge. However, I was relieved when the taxi pulled into the motel parking lot, and I had arrived safely with a receipt for a taxi fare which would not be embarrassing.

The next test came around dinner-time with Dr. William P Samuels, Jr. on July 5th, 1975. Bill was in charge of PhD recruitment for Union Carbide and had previously given me a first interview in London. He had left word at the hotel that he and his wife would pick me up at 6:00 p.m. for an early dinner. As we left, Bill said that we were going to a very nice restaurant nearby. Then, curiously, we drove for about an hour on Interstate roads and highways. To my British mind, a restaurant that was about fifty miles away was not close. In England, I rarely traveled between Gillingham and the next town over, Chatham. They were only about a mile apart. This jarred my historical frame of reference for describing distances. However, when you are trying to be on your best behavior, you just remain silent and carry on.

Little did I know that my night out would provide two more opportunities that tested my ability to act confidently in situations that I had not previously encountered.

I knew that the easiest way to handle menu selections was to defer to your host and hostess and ask what they recommended. After that decision was made, the waitress asked about salad dressing. In England, salad dressing implied mayonnaise. Therefore, I replied confidently, "Yes please." She logically, but inexplicably asked, "What type?" I stalled for time. I asked, "What do you have?"

As she reeled off a long list, I listened carefully so that I could make a selection with confidence. French seemed the safest, because France was geographically close to England.

The final test involved etiquette. Before dinner was served, the waitress placed an unusual decoration on our table — a tray of upright spring onions that looked like trees, which were surrounded by several other vegetables. Because I was perplexed, I watched my host and hostess. To my amazement, they ate vegetables from the tray. I simply followed suit, passed this test and was offered the job.

Whenever I don't know what to do, I quietly ponder options. Then, inevitably, I receive inspiration about what is an appropriate next step. In so doing, I avoid being flustered and am better able to proceed in a way that portrays confidence. I keep calm and carry on.

7. Baby It's Cold Outside

Ice Bridge – Niagara Falls, NY (Barker)

Being poised had helped me secure a job in a suburb of Buffalo, New York. However, as many people in the United States know, Buffalo has a newsworthy reputation of having particularly cold, snowy and dangerous winters. My first winter, the *Blizzard of 77*, was headline news in the US and also England. Because I grew up in London, I had no reference point to prepare me for surviving unbelievably low wind chills. I vividly recall needing to run as fast as I could from a car to the apartment (UK: flat), in order to avoid freezing to death.

According to the history books, Wind chills reached 50 to 60 degrees below zero. An unfathomable 199.4 inches of snow fell – beating the previous record by 73 inches (National Weather Service).

Sadly, the local newspaper (Warner) reported that twenty-nine people lost their lives. Some froze to death, immersed in blinding and disorientating snow.

Upon arriving home, immediately after I had unlocked the front door, I rushed to the thermostat and turned up the heat. I felt chilled to the bone. It took about two hours to feel warm again. The drive home had also been memorable. We frequently could not see the road ahead of us. At times, the gusting winds caused the snow to completely obscure our field of vision as the flakes were propelled horizontally.

This experience provided a stark contrast to winters in London where any snowfall was extremely rare. The Gulf Stream from the Florida coastline becomes the North Atlantic Drift. This bathes the shores of Cornwall and Devon in southern England with warm water. Despite the fact that London's latitude is about four degrees further north than St. John's Newfoundland, palm trees grow in Torquay, Devon.

Southern England was ill equipped to deal with snow. As a young child, I remember seeing a worker standing at the edge of the back of a lorry (US: truck) with a mound of sand behind him. He somehow managed to maintain his balance as he shoveled grit onto the glazed and slippery road while the lorry moved forward at a slow pace. One time, I remember that London shut down for about a week because six inches of snow had fallen.

During another particularly bitterly cold winter in Buffalo, I was driving to a meeting when my car started to lose power on the highway. I managed to pull over onto the hard shoulder – it was extremely dark. I tried to restart the car without success. The breakdown pre-dated cell phones, and I was not a member of the Automobile Association. In the distance I could see a gas station - on the other side of two embankments and a fence. I could see an area where the fence appeared to be broken down. Therefore, I thought that my best course of action was to walk towards the gas station and use a pay phone to call a friend to get advice. Perhaps this decision was unwise but made sense at the time.

As I started to quickly walk down one side of the relatively steep embankment, I realized that the valley was filled with exceptionally deep snow. I started to sink rapidly and had the startling thought that I might not be able to climb out of the snowdrift because it was too deep. Perhaps the darkness would make it unlikely for anyone to find me. This wasn't a particularly good situation in which to find myself. Overcoming the temptation to panic, I continued and clawed my way up the other side.

I survived and was happy to have learned something. At work my colleague said, "How can you see a silver lining? You could have died." My response was, "That's the point. I realized that I don't have any fear of dying."

He was concerned about the expense. I then remembered that my insurance policy included towing. The car dealership fixed the problem at no cost to me because they accepted responsibility after I pointed out that servicing a week earlier had probably precipitated the breakdown.

Perhaps I could have avoided finding myself in harm's way if I had considered my answer to the question that I am frequently asked, "Why did you ever decide to move from London to Buffalo?" However, even after enduring particularly harsh winters, my answer is always, "A unique opportunity presented itself for me to continue doing the research which I loved to do. My parents were in agreement. I have no regrets. In fact, my life has been enriched by the experience."

Buffalo is certainly much colder and snowier than London. In England, there are two seasons, winter just has more rain. Buffalo has four distinct seasons. Spring has always been exhilarating, because I am reminded that winter doesn't last forever.

By nature, I am intensely analytical. Before making any decision, it is always good for me to lay aside any preconceived notions. In the case of the move to Buffalo, I had no comparable frame of reference concerning winter. This did not matter to me, because I was more guided by an intrinsic and exceptionally motivating passion to perform research and development. Location was not a factor. There were not enough hours in the day to consider every possibility and eventuality.

After moving to Richmond, I still enjoy wearing shorts when it is bright and sunny but cold by Virginia standards. There have been times when cashiers enquire as to whether I am aware of the current outside temperature. I enjoy smiling and saying, "I used to live in Buffalo." No more needs to be said.

8. All Wet

Swimming Lesson – Rupert, Idaho (Russell)

After traversing the big pond, my life would be further enriched by teaching myself how to swim. Unlike the boys above, my first encounter with an instructor was far less idyllic.

A gruff portly man at the Latchmere Public Pool bellowed out commands that were designed to help us to get started. In my case, the effect was to drink large amounts of water, have experiences where I thought I was drowning and to develop a strong but unhealthy fear of drowning. This fear was not as debilitating as aquaphobia but was unnecessary and restricting.

During the first quarter century of my life, I had no desire to fall into water. As I walked up and down the gangways to embark and to disembarked from the Dover (Kent) to Calais

(France) ferries, I always chose to avoid looking down at the water that separated the ferryboat from the quay. Curiously, I could look at the English Channel from a distance, but never wanted to focus on water close at hand. Perhaps it was the sense of the potential for imminent danger and death. Perhaps it was the memory of my initial foray into the world of swimming instruction.

The point came in my life when I realized that it would be beneficial to set aside irrational fears, think logically and attempt to rise above previously debilitating fears.

As an engineer, I knew that if you kept your mouth closed, the natural tendency for the body would be to float. It is basically a matter of physics. The average density of a person is around 0.98 and the density of water is 1.0. A cork floats very well because its density is about 0.24. Therefore, theoretically I could just float and not drown – provided that I did not panic.

A second revelation came when I revisited my first encounter with the instructor. The memories of the traumatic experience continued to linger. At an intellectual level I knew that he was doing what he thought was best. However, this approach had not imparted the required confidence needed to learn how to swim. Because the disquiet inside me did not go away, I wondered if I was unwittingly holding onto resentment and bitterness towards the teacher. Therefore, it seemed appropriate to say a prayer to forgive him and ask that I could somehow become detached from the past memories and emotions from that first encounter with swimming pool instruction.

The first tangible step towards allaying my fears came after I had started working in the USA and had moved into Raintree Island Apartments in Tonawanda. They had an outdoor pool. For some unexplainable reason, I thought that perhaps I could learn how to float on water. On a regular basis, I would swim after work. The lifeguard occasionally gave me some pointers on how to float and encouraged me to learn swim strokes. The day I was able to float on my back and complete a lap provided such a sense of accomplishment and exhilaration. Periodically, I would live on the wild side and propel myself up and down the pool for many lengths on my back. I was not ready to risk taking in mouthfuls of water.

My wife was surprised to learn that I did not know how to swim. It seemed that she was amused by the analytic approach I had taken to conquer fear. Therefore, to help me along, she went to the local library and took out books on swimming that were of a similar vintage to the time when I had tried to learn how to swim in England. Finally, the day came when I flipped over and swam with my head facing the water.

That moment, when action and persistence triumphed over fear opened up a love for the water. Family vacations when we stayed in my wife's parents' cottage on Lake Michigan provided abundant opportunities to swim in cold water. The weather could be sunny or there could be strong waves that invited jumping into. The scene near the National Park Service's Sleeping Bear Dunes was idyllic and had a similar natural appearance to that shown in the picture above. I had found a love for the water and had been freed from past inhibitions.

Swimming now provides me with an excellent antidote for life's stresses. I regularly receive tangible benefits when my heart rate increases, more oxygen flows to my brain and I am sufficiently relaxed to allow thoughts and perspectives to unfold in my mind.

Previously, large bodies of water triggered irrational thinking. The fear of drowning was debilitating. Now, I have the confidence and knowledge to put such potentially tormenting fear in its place. That same liberating mindset helps me to remain standing after potentially overwhelming waves of life approach. I anticipate the thrill of jumping waves. They do not engulf me.

In my childhood, I was indeed all wet. My thoughts and feelings about water were wrong because of a difficult first encounter with a swimming instructor. Just like my Dad, I used rational thought, books and practice to teach myself. After I put past hang-ups in their place, I could make swimming one of my favorite forms of exercise. I became a person who loved and at times perhaps was addicted to swimming. The other day, I talked to a friend who was making travel arrangements. He said that I had taught him that one of the most important things to look for in a hotel was a swimming pool.

A wonderful but completely unanticipated consequence of knowing how to swim came when I experienced the thrill of teaching my children to swim. Because my life no longer remained stymied by the past, I was not robbed of the enormous pleasure of passing on my love of swimming. Fantastic is an apt word to describe my feelings as I saw the excitement in each of my daughters' eyes when they realized that they were swimming without help.

9. Steal my Purse

Piccadilly Circus – London (Detroit Publishing Company)

Good name in man and woman, dear my lord,
Is the immediate jewel of their souls;
Who steals my purse steals trash; 'tis something, nothing;
'twas mine, 'tis his, and has been slave to thousands;
(Shakespeare, "Othello")

Shakespeare's quote provides a healthy perspective. Some things can't be stolen, such as the priceless joy associated with teaching my daughters how to swim. However, on four occasions I recovered from the temporary disquiet precipitated by theft. The first incident involved witnessing a crime that unfolded in front of the building shown in the print above.

My whole family was in England during one of our annual trips to visit my Mum and Dad. As we were almost being carried along in the crowd, we saw the crime being executed. The victim had a backpack with an unzipped pocket and a camera that was partially visible. A very tall man cut in front of us without missing a beat and lifted the camera from its insecure moorings. Then he passed off the stolen goods to a second man who passed the camera to a third man. Everything happened in the twinkling of an eye. We continued to be pushed along by the crowd. We could no longer see the victim or remember what the criminals looked like.

I had a ringside seat to witness how quickly and proficiently well-organized criminals can execute their task. I had seen a vivid demonstration of the frequently touted benefit of hiding valuables to reduce temptation. However, as you will see later, taking this precaution did not protect me from theft.

Growing up, I was quite naïve. Once, I heard of a single instance when a schoolmate knew someone from our school who had confessed to shoplifting at the local Woolworths. The reality that thieves existed came to fore when I was shopping in that same store as a young teenager.

I was foraging through items in front of me when my eyes were attracted to a man who scanned the open counter furtively. Then he looked around, picked up and hid something underneath his coat. He quickly left the store. I was dumbfounded.

This raised my awareness that criminals existed and showed the importance of being aware of my surroundings. This helped to avoid being pickpocketed but didn't prevent my home burglary.

Anyone who has ever been burglarized knows the intensity of the thoughts and feelings when you receive news that your home has been broken into. Because I was at college,

I lived with three others in the low cost but rough London neighborhood of the Elephant & Castle. I did not own anything of particular monetary value. However, I had a keen sense of feeling violated as I assessed the scope of the crime and pondered the reality that a thief had recently foraged through my possessions.

The close inspection revealed that the thieves had stolen my collection of LP's (Long Play 33 vinyl records), and an electric shaver. Although not prone to being overly sentimental, I was a little sad when I realized that the theft had included several records that were presents from my Dad. My rational side quickly took over. I reasoned that things can always be replaced. I could have used the words of Shakespeare above, *twas mine, 'tis his.*

The police detective took one of my roommates to a shop, which was a known criminal haunt. As the detective entered, he said, "Don't bother getting up." He went on to say, "There has been a recent theft of records, and other items. Please let us know if someone tries to fence these items." The group which included recently released prisoners said that of course they would help. The detective quipped, "Of course, they won't. However, the next time they see the lads, they will box their ears. It will make it a little more difficult for the teenagers to sell stolen goods."

Happily, within the week, my roommate caught a glimpse of my records in a nearby secondhand shop. The police helped me recover my treasured records. The razor was never found.

Because I have seen crimes and have been a victim of crime, I try to reduce the number of temptations I present to criminals. Past thefts made me wonder if I should stop at a health club to swim before driving to a business meeting at which I needed my laptop. Heeding the insight learned in Piccadily Circus, I knew what would be my standard operating procedure. On arrival, I placed the computer out of view in the trunk (UK: Boot), but I didn't known I was being watched. After I had left the car, there had been a *crash and grab theft*. The driver's window was broken, the trunk unlocked and the laptop stolen. On the bright side, insurance pays to replace things and backups help restore data and programs effortlessly.

Being cautious is a good thing, but I am constantly reminded of my experiences and the advice given by a British Policeman. He said that when you park a car you can take precautions that will reduce the risk of it being stolen. You can park underneath a street light, and you can install a steering wheel lock. Despite taking such precautions, the reality is that for a professional thief anything you do will provide little deterrence value if they want to steal your car. They only will be slowed down a little. A joy rider might be deterred and move onto the next car which is easier to borrow.

I try to be careful. However, this provided no guarantees. The best way to safeguard my heart was to develop the correct attitude towards possessions. They can come, and they can also go.

The bonus is that the London Metropolitan Police helped me to continue to enjoy the records that my Dad gave me. Even if the records had never been recovered, no thief can ever take away the good name that my Dad has given me.

10. On a Wing and a Prayer

C-47 Transport Plane Landing Gear – Long Beach, CA (Palmer)

The picture above reminds me of my Dad's WW II service and the stories he told me about travelling in military transport planes. While he worked in intelligence, he collected and analyzed news clippings. His love of news was passed onto me.

A few years ago, I was mesmerized as I watched the TV report about the potential disaster facing a JetBlue Airbus and its 141 passengers (Hradecky). My mind and emotions returned to a similar experience about twenty-five years before. The events, experiences and end result were similar. However, technological advances had dramatically changed how the story was reported, changing the impact on those involved, and upon their loved ones.

On September 22nd, 2005, reporters brought the reality faced by passengers on the JetBlue plane into the living rooms of the world. The JetBlue plane had taken off from Berkley en route for New York. At takeoff, the landing gear had stayed locked at 90 degrees. Interestingly, this broadcast was also beamed to the passengers on-board, who could watch live streaming satellite television and hear their plight described. One passenger, Zachery Mastoon from New York, later called the experience "surreal" (Associated Press). Shortly before the Airbus 230 attempted to land, the TV feed was turned off (Leovy).

The Airbus passengers had to embrace the reality that their plane could land without the correct functioning of the landing gear. This raised the potential that the aircraft could land and catch on fire – with a high probability of death. Thankfully, in the end, the plane landed safely.

A TV commentator provided the following trigger for my trip back down memory lane, when he asked the question, "I wonder what the passengers are thinking and feeling?" From personal experience, I could hazard a guess because I remember what I was thinking during a similar incident.

My experience was on an Air Canada Boeing Jumbo Jet flying between Los Angeles Airport and Toronto Pierson Airport. About twenty minutes before arriving, a friend who was an off duty Air Canada pilot observed that something was going on. A few minutes later, the Captain announced that the landing gear could collapse on landing, but there was nothing to worry about. Immediately, the air grew tense as passengers considered the worst-case scenario.

Calmly, the Captain announced that it would be necessary to follow emergency landing procedures.

Shortly after this, a passenger had to receive an oxygen breathing apparatus. My travelling companion suggested that we pray for the passengers who contemplated an uncertain future.

The question that came to my mind was, "Is this my time?" It seemed that there were many more things that I believed I was supposed to do in life. However, there were no guarantees that I would escape unharmed.

The crew efficiently came through the cabin to pick up any remaining cups and wrappers. We were instructed to take off our eyeglasses and brace for the landing. As we hit the ground, I looked out of the window and noticed a whole flotilla of fire engines and ambulances driving at breakneck speed to keep up with the plane. Their fire hoses were at the ready, pointing at the plane. My first, but silly, question was, "I wonder why they are there?" Thankfully, we landed and without incident.

What I learned next gave me pause for thought. When my friend Ian picked me up, I shared the story. He found it very interesting because a mutual friend from Buffalo, New York had woken up at 2:00 a.m. and felt the need to pray for my safety.

Years later, Marjorie, who was a friend from England, told me that she usually prayed for me every day at 7:00 a.m. Because she knew I travelled a lot, she usually prayed for my safety. After she told me this, a light went on in my mind; if you allow for time differences, it was not inconceivable that they had both prayed the same thing for me at precisely the same moment.

Thankfully, my adventure ended safely. However, whenever there is a tragic event involving a plane, I comfort myself by reflecting on flight safety statistics. For example, following a recent crash in the Swiss Alps, *Forbes Magazine* put the probability of death in a commercial airliner at 1 in 7 million (Lane). This can be compared to 1 in 88,000 for dying in a bicycle accident.

My attitude to flying is similar to my Mum's attitude while she was dodging Hitler's bombing of London. She said, "If my name was on a bomb, it will find me."

Perhaps that mindset is why I flew across the Atlantic shortly after the downing of the Lockerbie Pan Am Flight 103 on December 21st, 1988. Security was certainly tight when I arrived at Heathrow Airport with burly police officers openly carrying sub-machine guns and escorted by extremely large dogs.

I also took advantage of the incredibly low transatlantic fares following the 9-11 September 11th, 2001 attack on the World Trade Towers in New York City. For $275 including all taxes and fees, I made a round trip to Rome, Italy with a stopover in London. Also provided was a free hotel accommodation for the first night in Rome, and my ticket could be changed without penalty.

When it comes to flying, I am faced with the decision about whether my actions should be constrained by fear, or I should be adventurous and journey forth in faith. Faith wins over fear.

My brush with a potentially serious problem of collapsed landing gear has taught me that when you fly it's usually best to travel on a wing and a prayer.

11. A Sticky Wicket

Cricket Action – Lynmouth, Devon (McGowan)

When the pilot in the previous chapter tried to land, he was figuratively caught playing on a sticky wicket which the Oxford Dictionary of Phrase and Fable defines as follows:

> A cricket pitch that has been drying after rain and is difficult to bat on; a tricky or awkward situation. The term is recorded in its literal sense from 1882, in a reference to the Australians finding themselves on a sticky wicket; the first figurative example is found in the 1950s. (Knowles)

Tricky and awkward are appropriate adjectives to describe the challenges my wife and I faced as we owned a multi-tenant office building. Despite difficulties, we always went to bat.

On July 7th, 1998, my wife and I purchased a 4,500 sq. ft. dilapidated commercial property through foreclosure. The building was home to my computer consultancy business.

As anyone in business knows, the economy has the annoying habit of causing downturns. This happened to me, following on the heels of buying the building with all its attendant expenses.

Shortly after becoming owners, we needed to resolve the problem of a leaking roof which was beyond repair. When faced with a difficult situation, my first reaction is to always identify the options that might bring resolution to the problem at hand. In the case of the roof, I talked with a contractor who explained that the best long-term solution was to replace the existing flat roof with a sloping hip roof. This would have the lowest cost of ownership because it required the least amount of maintenance. The best course of action had been identified, but the financial resources were not available. Imagine our relief when there was a distribution from an inheritance that arrived just in time to contract for the roof reconstruction. The builder only had a single, extremely narrow, three day time slot in which to complete our project. Immediately after completion of the roofing project, he left on vacation. On his return, he would face a completely booked year of new home construction projects. Timing is everything.

About five years later we faced another financial challenge – possible foreclosure for non-payment of property taxes. More large expenses had further depleted our resources. Erie County had sent us a final demand notice for payment by close of business on October the 31st. What should we do? The clock ticked on.

Knowing what to do was simple. I just needed to find money. The source of the funds was the issue. I had no immediate ideas about the source for such a large amount of additional revenue.

My wife joked, "Perhaps we need a fish with a coin in its mouth." I looked at her quizzically. She continued, "The Lord supernaturally provided a coin so that his disciples could pay Caesar the taxes which were due him."

Curiously, my wife's words came to mind, when I talked with one of my software sales representatives in England. Jane and Barry were a husband and wife team who marketed the Super Sort software utility to companies based in the United Kingdom. For many years, they had faithfully sent modest but regular payments to the United States. Then, suddenly the flow of money stopped.

When I enquired as to the reason, they told me that they believed that the software developer, who had previously purchased licenses, still used the program but no longer purchased them. The new purchasing agent at the software development company seemed far less meticulous than her predecessor. She had not placed an order in a long time. When they tried to follow up with her, she would never return their calls. Their feeling was that the client was using the software without the legal right to do so. However, Jane and Barry felt that it didn't make economic sense for either of our businesses to pursue additional action. Reluctantly, I agreed, but emotionally, it felt so wrong.

If the software developer was indeed stealing software, I believed that there would be consequences. However, in such a case, I would not be the person who should or could administer justice.

Then, I felt inspired to send the software developer a letter that touched on the issue of the surprising downturn in orders. Shortly afterwards, Jane called from England. She said that Barry and she had talked and were of the opinion that it might be worthwhile to make one more pitch to the developer. They suggested offering a one-time purchase of an unlimited license agreement. They were flabbergasted when the developer quickly agreed to place an order despite repeated rebuffs in the past. Of course, the size of the order would be sufficient to pay the tax bill. Our concerted effort had resulted in a sale. Just because the invoice was printed, payment was not guaranteed. In addition, I had no control over when the net proceeds would be available in the USA.

As foreclosure action loomed, I waited. The client sent payment to Jane and Barry. Once the funds cleared, Jane mailed a check to me. I waited. The bank platform officers did not know how long it would take for such a foreign check to clear. Would the funds clear in time? All I could do was wait, and wait some more.

On the morning of the last day of October, I confirmed that the funds were available. I drove to the Erie County cashier's office with the required payment. At 4:00 p.m., I joined others who also stood in line on October the 31st. We all knew why we were there. The office was open until 4:30 p.m. After the taxes were paid, our checking account had 11 cents. Being in the black is always good.

Although property ownership has repeatedly necessitated that we face an uncertain future, we have never shrunk back. We have always been willing to go to bat. We had no control on how the ball would spin, but it was usually in the right direction.

12. Anne

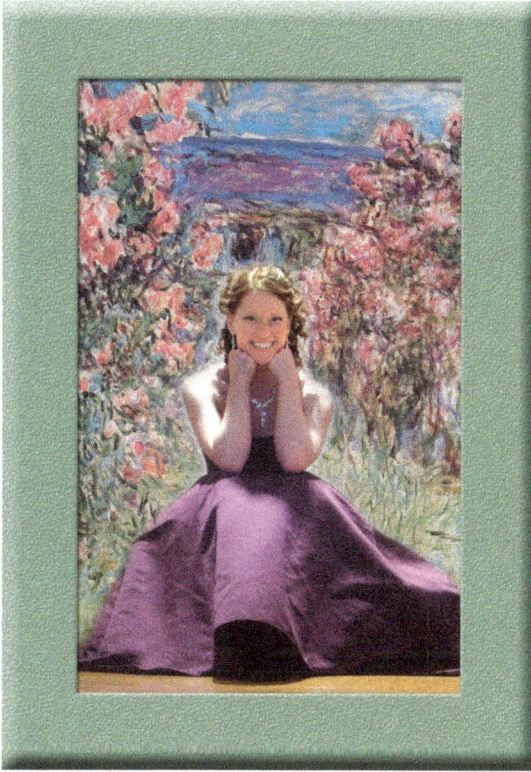

Anne Elisabeth Jackson (Jackson, April 2010)

All the world's a stage,
And all the men and women merely players;
They have their exits and their entrances.

(Shakespeare, "As you Like it")

Life can throw you a curveball that bounces in a completely unanticipated direction. Would the one that was thrown at me take me out of the game or would it help me to become a better player? The outcome would depend upon my response and my perspective.

Many people have expressed how much they enjoy viewing the photograph at the beginning of this chapter. In

April of 2010, I snapped this picture at Nyack College. My daughter Anne had just performed her fantastic Junior Recital. Later that year, a talented and creative artist from Buffalo thought that my picture and Claude Monet's *House Among the Roses* could work well together. I think that you will agree that his composition is beautiful. The perspective evokes the tension of seeing Anne enjoying life fully, but behind her is a sense of the ethereal with its own implicit beauty.

Anne's dreams and aspirations were shortly going to be shattered. Her family and friends were going to be left with only the fragments and fragrance of her short life on earth.

On November the 17th, my wife and I listened to a call that no parent ever wants to get. Penny, Nyack College's athletic trainer told us that Anne was running and fell, and was currently in the emergency room at Nyack Community Hospital.

Later, I would find out that a doctor at the hospital had called the New York State Troopers. She had asked if they could escort us during our unscheduled three hundred and sixty mile trip from Buffalo to Nyack. The Troopers told her that they did not do that. She told them about the circumstances and asked them not to give us a ticket if we were speeding. We tried to pace ourselves emotionally and mentally and used cruise control to pace the car.

Finally, in the early hours of the 18th, we arrived at the hospital. The staff stood silently and rigidly at full attention. I had an intense sinking feeling and a keen sense of foreboding. They ushered us towards the attending physician who broke the news.

The emergency room doctor explained that Anne had collapsed while running, and that for about an hour, two cardiologists had tried to save her life. Sadly our beloved daughter never made it through this last trial of her life. No longer could a room be lit up with her smile and by her encouraging words.

We later found out that a virus had attacked our twenty one year old daughter's heart, and Anne had experienced heart failure. There was no history of symptoms that one would associate with such a heart condition. Also, there was no family history of cardiomyopathy.

The sudden unanticipated death of Anne could have shaken my faith. My wife and I had heard of situations in which marriages fell apart following similar events. I had no prior frame of reference to use as a basis to process such a sudden and dramatic event. Recently, a friend messaged me:

> I need to ask you a question about your reaction to the loss
> ... I want to specifically hone in on the issue of 'What kind
> of God would allow this to happen?'

I asked myself, "How would I articulate my reply to such a difficult question?"

Being able to completely understand and judge such an event would presuppose that I possessed an infinite repository of knowledge. I'm exceptionally grateful that the completion of a research PhD from a premier world university revealed the fallacy in that belief. After being awarded my doctorate at age 24, I came to a startling but exceptionally liberating intellectual revelation. I recognized how very little I knew about one part of one subject at one university. Therefore, how could I be qualified to judge God regarding my daughter's death? It was above my paygrade.

Knowing the impact of the loss of a loved one upon a marriage, Judy, a senior pastor at a large church in Lancaster (NY), asked Cindy, "How did you and Gordon ever get through such a tragedy?" Cindy answered:

> Early on, we realized that we needed to hear and to comfort each other. However, we had to process feelings individually. We each needed to obtain our own peace.

Sometimes, I use the following analogy to describe the new perspective that has been birthed in me. When I cross the road, I might be hit by a car. I will use care when crossing. If I see the car coming, I will try to avoid being hit. However, the reality is that on any day and at any time I could become another fatality statistic. That is not being morbid. It's a simple fact. I need to live each day to the fullest. This has translated into a simpler life, lived with greater spontaneity and consequential richness. I can make bold decisive moves, and I am free to explore new avenues of interest.

After operating my own computer consultancy for thirty-three years, the defining event of November the 17th showed me that I would benefit from a change. I closed the business, moved five hundred miles and returned to University in order to teach. Also, I no longer needed to be constrained by the chains of scientific and technical writing. I could learn how to write creatively.

Anne would never have wanted her death to be a showstopper. She embodied the adage the show must go on.

13. Love Is All You Need

University of Pennsylvania – Philadelphia PA (Vinocur)

Sometimes, to keep the show continuing, we need to be encouraged. How? In the words of the Beatles song:

> All you need is love
> All you need is love
> All you need is love, love
> Love is all you need (Lennon)

Through an act of kindness, love often becomes tangible. When it comes to helping children survive and prosper, it invariably *Takes a Village* (Clinton). That was certainly true for a pretty little girl in the Dominican Republic who lived a bleak existence. She lived at a level of poverty few of us can imagine. The surroundings did little to cheer her up.

One day, George Bolduc, an American Missionary, arrived in her village with a big smile on his face. He carried an army surplus duffle bag (UK: Kit bag). She did not know that there was a gift inside that bag sent from someone who wanted her to be touched by love. George rummaged through the bag doing his own imitation of Santa Claus and presented the little girl with a beautiful gently used dress. Whenever she wore this treasure, she was overjoyed. Finally she felt that someone in the world loved her. That simple loving act lifted her spirits and gave her hope.

The story behind the dress began several months before. My wife and I were going through some particularly turbulent financial times in business. Money was exceptionally tight. However, we had learned that whenever monetary resources were scant, our circumstances would change when we focused on others. This was often extremely difficult because we had to dredge up sufficient cash to make our heart-felt expression of love tangible.

We knew that George made regular missionary trips to the Dominican Republic. When we had asked him about how we could be involved, he suggested that we buy duffle bags, fill them with presentable lightly used clothes and then send them to him via the Postal Service. Because he lived in Puerto Rico, the shipping cost would be the same as the domestic rate. Even though the shipment was sent by air, we only had to pay the ground rates, which was only $8. However, this often seemed like a large sum of money because our resources were so limited.

The fact that my wallet only contained moths was insufficient to deter us from filling a duffle bag with clothes and placing the bag in the trunk of my car. We would wait until such time as we were able to eke out sufficient funds to send our contribution on its way. Generally, this happened within about a week of preparing the shipment. Shortly after we dispatched our modest gift, there would always be an increase in our cash flow. Sometimes it was something as simple as a customer paying a past-due bill. Regardless of our situation, we realized that within our personal constraints, we needed to show love to others who had a much greater need than ours. We felt compelled to give out of our lack.

Many years later, I met George and he asked me, "Did I ever tell you what happened to one of the dresses you had sent me?"

My curiosity raised, I answered, "No."

George continued, "A few years after I had given that beautiful dress to a little girl, I revisited her family. She had worn the dress for about six months, and then had outgrown it. With excitement and emotion, she beckoned me to follow her and pulled out that same dress from underneath her mattress. Your gift had meant so much to her."

Immediately I returned home, I shared George's story with my wife. We both cried. Our daughter had received the dress as a gift. We had passed on something that was no longer of value to our family. The US Postal Service carried it about 1,800 miles to Puerto Rico. George took it to the Dominican Republic. The recipient had been touched by much needed love, and so had we. This certainly reinforces the notion that survival does indeed take a village.

Both my wife and I naturally tend to enjoy giving. Whenever we do so, we feel blessed. However, there are times when we have needed to be on the receiving end of the love that others willingly shared with us.

A few years after I had started my first business, I found myself with a car that didn't work, and insufficient funds to cover the repair costs. I was a part of a business association, and could only muster sufficient energy to call one of the members. His particular skill-set included car repair. My situation caused me to feel overwhelmed. After a brief talk, Sunny asked where the car was located. Then he said, "Consider it done." The group took up a collection to pay for the parts. A week later, I had transportation again and was able to be back in business all thanks to Sunny.

Bill, another dear friend, invariably discerns from my countenance when I am in need of help, especially for property maintenance and repair. I have lost count of the number of times he has willingly volunteered, by asking, "When do you need me to come? ... How long do you want me to stay? ... Do you need me to come tomorrow?" For some reason, he usually offers to help during times that require significant physical labor. Both of us feel the effects, because we are not as young as we once were. Bill is like the brother I never had and has even provided a literal shoulder on which to cry. His acts of service in some pretty grungy situations send the palpable message of love and appreciation.

An impoverished girl regained hope through the love of my wife and myself. Our situations were bearable because of the love we received. It often takes a village to demonstrate the reality that all you need is love.

14. Showing Up

CACC Cross Country Championships – Philadelphia, PA (Jackson)

In the previous chapter, the Dominican girl's spirit was raised by a tangible gift. I was told that the spirits of the cross country runners shown above are further raised by the messages I have shared during the awards ceremonies at the NCAA Cross Country Championships. Although showing up wasn't always easy, Woody Allen has said, "Showing up is eighty percent of life (Allen)."

Since 2011, my wife and I have been invited to Beaumont Plateau in Philadelphia's Fairmount Park. We have been afforded the honor presenting the cross country team sportsmanship awards at the NCAA Division II Central Atlantic Collegiate Conference Cross Country Championships.

Considering our lack of sports acumen and prowess, this assignment seems quite astonishing.

It has often been difficult to muster sufficient strength to show up. The first year was exceptionally challenging.

We had accepted the assignment of presenting the Women's Cross Country Team Sportsmanship award to Nyack College. The award had been renamed to honor our daughter, Anne Elisabeth Jackson, who had collapsed at a meet the previous autumn and had died.

The NCAA Division II Commissioner, Dan Mara, assured us that our daughter exemplified the scholar athlete who understood and modeled genuine sportsmanship.

Attending that first championship event was both bitter and sweet. We were glad that our daughter was being honored but intensely sad that she was no longer present to enjoy that moment.

As the day approached, my wife and I had an understandable sense of foreboding. We were not certain how we would be able to get through the day, maintaining a positive outlook, which could be an inspiration to the athletes. As the hour to leave our hotel room for the championships approached, I assured my wife that it was completely acceptable for her to remain at the hotel. I felt that I would somehow manage to be able to present the awards.

Putting emotions aside, we both believed that our attendance at the event would encourage those who had been touched by our daughter's sudden death. Our implicit message from being present would be that regardless of what happens, it is always a healthy course of action to continue on with one's life. In the end, my wife felt strong enough to accompany me. My spoken address emphasized the heartfelt reality that sometimes we do not want to show up. However, it is often important to do so. We felt that our presence encouraged others to regain a balanced perspective.

The next year, I read a jolting social media posting about Rob Roman, a cross-country runner from the Post University Eagles. Post is in the same NCAA championship conference as is Nyack. The runner had collapsed during a cross-country meet at Beaumont and had died about a week later. Emotionally, I was instantaneously transported back to the intensity of the moments that surrounded the death of our daughter a few years before. Tears gushed as I contemplated the past. This was a few days before the next championship meet. Sensing the potential impact of the sudden death on me, Commissioner Dan Mara asked Nyack's Athletics Trainer to call me. I saw her number displayed on my mobile phone, accepted the call and was happy to hear her cheery voice, "Hello, this is Penny. How are you doing?" My honest response was, "Not particularly well." I could feel that her heart went out to me. She continued, "Commissioner Mara asked me to call, because he realizes that recent events may make it particularly difficult for you to attend the upcoming championships."

My response was immediate, "The commissioner's sensitivity touches me. I might be a basket case before the meeting, and a basket case afterwards. However, I believe that I will be able to gather the strength and presence of mind to present the awards. I think that it is highly unlikely that I will not show up." Penny knew me well, and said, "I completely understand."

When the day came, I was not only able to present the awards but was afforded the opportunity to share encouraging words with the team that had been impacted by the death.

Before the meet, I talked with Dan the Commissioner and said that I would like to meet Post University's coach and let him know that he was in my thoughts and prayers. Dan told me that he would arrange for this to happen. Between the Men's and Women's championships, Dan came over to fetch me. He said that this would be a good time to meet the coach, so he walked me across the field.

In the distance I could see all the Post University team members and coaches looking in my direction. I had not envisioned such a formal contact and wondered what I should say. As I approached them, their faces betrayed the reality that they had been touched by death.

In those short poignant moments, we were all close to tears. To provide emotional relief, I shared this story:

> I used to think that cross-country and track were similar. I now know the difference between a marathon and a sprint. Thankfully, when I used the wrong term, the cross-county community forgave me. Now that I know better, I no longer confuse the two sports.

We all laughed, shook hands and hugged. Perhaps I helped them feel that they were not alone in their grief.

The next year, my wife and I were given our own his and hers Cross Country Championship watches. In high school, athletics was never my forte. If you had told me that I would receive a cross-county award, I would have thought that you were off your nut.

We have consistently been empowered to go. Facing the decision about going has never been easy. Whenever we show up, the faces of the athletes always express heartfelt appreciation.

15. Stepping Stones

Bodies in Motion – Bolton Abbey, Skipton, N Yorkshire (Stevensen)

During a trip down memory lane concerning career development, I identified four defining moments when business as usual came to a logical stopping point. The status quo no longer worked. It was time for me to take another step.

The picture above rekindles thoughts and feelings about those times of change. Reticence? Fear? Youthful confidence about stretching? A need for a realistic identification of my core competencies? Willingness to receive a helping hand?

Once I heard it said, "It is a form of insanity to keep doing the same thing and to expect different results." Therefore to remain sane, I have already used four different career stepping stones. How many more career stepping stones will I need? Some consider that seven is common, while others consider that such a figure is too high (Bialik). I wonder how many more changes will happen in my life.

Natural inquisitiveness and an ability to study provided my starting point. Books were my friends. However, when

I read *The Element* (Robinson), I discovered that one of the Beatles, Ringo Starr, blossomed after he pushed his books aside. His first stepping stone was listening to rock music and learning how to play the guitar. As Robinson said, "Finding your passion changes everything."

My first step was self-motivated. As an A-type teenager, I wrote to the Institution of Chemical Engineers in England and decided that chemical engineering would be my chosen field of study. Further research and the respect my Dad had for Imperial College in London made my choice easy.

About a year before I obtained an honors degree in chemical engineering, the job market dried up. As a result, most of my peers sought jobs in fields unrelated to their studies. As for myself, I had a hodge-podge of interviews. Unilever offered a management-training program. The Inland Revenue (US: IRS) was hiring tax inspectors. The Patent Office was hiring examiners. I applied to be a commissioned officer in the Royal Air Force. Nothing opened up.

With few job prospects and being young without any responsibilities, studying for a PhD provided a welcomed and unique opportunity to focus on research and satisfy a desire to keep learning. I was warmly welcomed by the brilliant Professor Roger Sargent. He held the Courtaulds' Chair of Chemical Engineering and had a keen research interest in computer applications before computer science departments existed in most universities. After four years, I happily completed my PhD, *"Interactive Chemical Plant Design."* This would be my second stepping stone.

While I had thoroughly enjoyed living in central London near Kensington Palace, I realized that the time was approaching when I should seek gainful employment. Interestingly, while I pondered this question I attended a party. One of the lecturers, Dr. James Noble asked, "Have you thought about working in America?" I replied, "No. Not really." He went on to say, "Union Carbide has some 'non-rubbish' jobs in the USA." He asked me if I was interested in working in America. I said that I did not know.

Then, one day, a fellow post-graduate, Brian Stokes stopped me shortly before lunch and said, "The chap from Union Carbide is here today. If you want it, you can have an interview at 3 p.m."

I returned to my residence halls and put on a suit. The interview went well.

My parents encouraged me in the belief that I would escape discrimination by moving to the US. In the bicentennial year, I found myself in the USA working in research and development. Union Carbide had obtained the required H-1B work permit for me.

By the late seventies, energy pricing brought disruption. Union Carbide was in turmoil. This frustrated me to the point that I resigned. I wanted to be responsible for my own destiny. My manager, Lou Batta, said:

> I admire you for deciding to become an entrepreneur. Several times, I've thought about doing that. As I get older, it's less likely. I guess I don't have the guts.

This didn't take guts. It was the simple recognition that the status quo wasn't working. I needed to take my third step.

I ran my computer consultancy for thirty-five years. However, a double-dip recession impacted me dramatically. I reached the point where I dreaded emails from paying clients because action would be needed. The status quo was no longer viable. My heart was no longer engaged in business, so I needed to find and to move on to the next stepping stone.

Towards the end of the life of the consulting business, it had become apparent to me that a change was in order. A good academic friend of mine strongly encouraged me to consider returning to the academic world. For about five years, I submitted applications to US and Canadian Universities. I applied for full-time and for adjunct appointments. Until a couple of years ago, the results were encouraging, but never led to an appointment.

Because of the events that have already been described, my wife and I knew that, once again, change was desirable and necessary for our long term health. It seemed that we should consider relocation. We still had enough energy to face the trauma of culling our possessions and moving house. With a little research, I concluded that moving from New York to Virginia might be a beneficial fifth step. I shifted my focus to academic establishments in the Virginia area. Again, there were openings but none turned into appointments, until one day my cell phone rang.

My wife and I were driving to Virginia for a holiday to help us decide upon the suitability of the area as our new domicile. I was asked to come in for an interview. To keep up appearances, I had to buy smart clothes for my interview. I was offered a full-time teaching position as a computer science professor, and I'm loving it.

16. A Track to Run On

Blackie Blasting out of the Tunnel – London, England (Hirkimer, 1960)

Conceptually, the transition to a teaching career would be a simple step. In practice, I needed to ride my figurative train.

The picture above reminds me of an early encounter on a steam train. My Mum had warned me about putting my head out of the window when a steam train was in a tunnel. She said, "Coal dust could get in your eye." I put my head out, and soot caused my eyes to water. Reason was trumped by my fascination with trains.

As a young child, I was an obsessive-compulsive train spotter. I would find vantage points from which to observe steam and diesel engines and use Ian Allan publications to record the engine numbers I had spotted. Sometimes these engines sped right past me on the platform where I was standing.

On a cold winter's day, I was traveling in upstate New York, between Buffalo and Albany. After the train left

Syracuse, I gazed outside at the white vista created by a blizzard. Visibility was almost zero. As the train climbed the hill, it slowed down to a crawl and then stopped. I was warm and safe. These words from a popular song came to mind:

> In every life we have some trouble
> But when you worry, you make it double
> Don't worry, be happy (McFerrin)

Later, I discovered that the diesel engine had lost traction. To help pull the carriages up the hill, a second engine was dispatched to the front. This provided insufficient traction, so a third engine was sent to push the train from the rear. We made it through. However, those who drove cars on the New York State Thruway had to seek refuge. It was one of the very few times in my memory when the Thruway was closed out of concern for drivers' safety.

Ultimately, I reached the destination despite the weather which caused exceptionally treacherous conditions for the motorists. Inside the comfortable train, I could look out at the wide white panoramic view and wonder how anyone would be able to navigate his or her way through such blinding snow. They couldn't.

The decision to ride the train to Albany was wise. I felt secure in the knowledge that the track to my destination was already in place for this trip, and I didn't have to try and drive.

In an analogous way, a recent complicated move from Buffalo to Richmond needed a figurative track to run on. My wife and I decided that she would stay in Buffalo, while I set up a beachhead in Richmond and drove back and forth.

There were complications. We owned a commercial property and a home, which both needed to be fixed up and sold. For decades, we had gathered possessions, which needed to be carefully culled, packed and moved. In addition, I did not yet have any accrued vacation time. Therefore, the required work would necessitate that I become a weekend home improvement warrior.

However, a round trip between Richmond and Buffalo is about a thousand miles. The default route according to my GPS involved taking Interstate 95 North and then navigate around Washington on the Beltway. In the unlikely event of there being no traffic on the Beltway, this would take the least amount of time. However, in order to ensure that this transition was completed successfully, I needed a better track on which to run.

With a careful study of the map, some experimentation, and flexibility at my place of employment, I created a routine. On Thursdays I would leave work as soon as possible after 1 p.m. Then I would zig and zag on roads to wend my way north to Buffalo, avoiding the Washington Beltway. At 8:00 a.m. each Monday, I needed to be back in the classroom. Perhaps, I was not always completely bright eyed and bushy tailed.

Once the route was established, I needed to concentrate on enjoying the ride. I listened to classical music and had frequent coffee breaks. Over time, the car seemed to know the way. It is difficult to believe that during this transitional period of about one year, I made twenty-four thousand mile weekend round-trips.

Recently as we drank coffee, we both sat in amazement as we remembered that some of the trips were taken on back-to-back weekends. Sometimes, accidents closed down the highways for hours. My wife mused, "How did you ever make it through?" I quipped, "One mile at a time."

Just like the train that made it through a blizzard, we also made it through the move. At times it felt like we were being pushed and pulled rather than driving under our own steam. We were comforted that there was a track to run on.

One of my daughters had observed my long-term driving marathon from a distance. When faced with regular but long weekend trips, she said to a friend, "My Dad, who is older than me, drove more than this. Therefore, I can also make the trips."

As I focus on the impact of trains on my life, I see that they continue to fascinate me. For my parents who never learned how to drive, trains were essential for travel to distant places. As a child with limited means, being close to trains helped me dream of the places they might take me one day. My childhood dreams were fulfilled when my parents rode trains during regular European holidays (US: Vacations). I can vividly recall the sense of wonder and amazement that accompanied waking up in a sleeper car to a sunrise view of the towering Swiss Alps in all their beauty and glory. Wonderful.

Today, my wife and I have a similar sense of amazement as we enjoy our new home. This became a reality because of our willingness to identify a track on which to run and then to figuratively climb on board and enjoy the ride. Are you ready to pack your bags and see where your train will take you?

17. Junk or Treasure?

Boot Sale – Tetsworth, Oxfordshire (Efekt)

Travel can be exciting, but the prospect of a move is often both exciting and daunting. Over decades, my wife and I purchased many things that were once treasures. But now?

There is some truth in the adage that my junk is someone else's treasure. However, it is difficult for me to put my possessions in the junk category. Any items I own are still valuable in my sight, even if they only provide an emotional tie to the past – the memories and associated enjoyment received from their ownership.

Despite the pleasure associated with the past, there are times when I have needed to move forward, and to scour the world in order to find good homes for my possessions. There has been a sense of enjoyment and satisfaction as I have found and pieced together the clues that would ultimately lead me to the individuals who were waiting for the opportunity to treasure my junk.

As a child, I treasured model railways. As soon as I was allowed to ride the bus alone, I made regular trips to the

Gamages department store in Holborn, London. The draw was their massive model railway display designed and built by Bertram Otto over a three year period. About one hundred trains moved between six countries nestled in the Alps. Platform announcements were made in different languages through tiny to-scale speakers. There was a tram, a cable car, an amusement park and even a monorail. I was always mesmerized when the lights in the exhibition hall dimmed and thousands of small lights glistened tantalizingly.

A fascination with railways combined with my inspirational trips to see Otto's display inspired me to pour most of my pocket and birthday money into purchasing enormous quantities of OO gauge Tri-ang engines, rolling stock, accessories and track. As soon as Lines Brothers introduced the integrated to-scale Minic Motorways, I went to the Arding and Hobbs department store in Clapham Junction to buy more accessories to increase the complexity of my layout, which gave me countless hours of pleasure. Who wouldn't want to be able to drive a scale model car onto a car transporter?

Then, forty years later, I lived in the United States and still owned and rented my parents' former home in Gillingham, Kent. Because the renter was also a good friend, he stored the boxes full of my childhood memories. The day came when the house was sold and the boxes had to find a new caring home.

Who could get the most benefit from the model railway set that had provided me with indescribable joy? A Google search for *"Model railways mission"* led me to an Anglican Vicar who used discarded model railways to raise money for charities that related to railways and children. He willingly accepted my donation. He fixed up and sold sets in order to raise money for *Railway Children*, a mission that befriends children who are at risk when they arrive at a London train terminus seeking a better life in the big city. What a wonderfully appropriate way for my clutter to become a treasure.

Sometimes the treasure for which you are responsible is inherited. Many years ago, my children accumulated an inordinate number of plush TY *Beanie Babies*. They were no longer emotionally connected to the toys. Unlike their Dad, they were happy to find a good home for their treasures – right away. Again, a Google search led me to a group that made annual mission trips to Ukranian schools. They drove a truck and distributed treasures to teachers and children who still remained in areas that after more than ten years were still contaminated by radiation that was released during the 1986 Chernobyl nuclear plant disaster in the Soviet Union.

The mission leaders in Great Britain gladly agreed to take the large numbers of soft, plushy stuffed animals for those children in need. My next challenge was to transport them from the USA to England. I wondered what the British Customs officer would think about a man of my age, arriving from America, carrying suitcases stuffed with Beanie Babies? Thankfully he didn't ask any questions.

Years earlier, I was faced with the wrenching decision concerning the correct way to dispose of comedy video tapes that had given much enjoyment to my Mum. The tape format would not work in standard US video players. I stopped, thought and remembered that studies had found that cancer patients benefited from laughter. The nearby Hospice was delighted to immediately run those dated but funny movies.

Our family's most recent move to south of the Mason-Dixon Line provided many opportunities to consider what should remain after downsizing. I found myself with many items that were too bulky, too heavy or unnecessary in our new location.

Not only had we gathered many possessions, but I still owned a very large quantity of serviceable but unused building materials and supplies. These were left over from years of home improvement projects and from the repairs and improvements necessary when you fix up a house to sell. Again, my thinking triggered a call to the local Habitat for Humanity store. They could sell my building supplies, hoses, large planters, lumber, plywood, partially full cans of paint and much more. My excess could be affordable for those in need, and Habitat's sales would subsidize other projects.

One of the last things that needed a new home before moving was a tall fiberglass a-frame ladder. I talked to a neighbor. He was still recovering from a stroke but seized the opportunity to become the custodian of the ladder for high painting jobs. He was touched and offered to mow the lawn when I was out of town.

Finally, our home was decluttered. We could move to Richmond with just fond memories of past treasures from two continents without the ongoing responsibility for their care.

To find homes for my junk, I simply ask the question, "Who could most benefit from owning this?" Inspiration and information always follow. Junk is transformed into treasure, and I find this outcome to be both therapeutic, and liberating.

18. On Her Majesty's Secret Service

1969 Mercury Cougar Convertible – Beaulieu, Hampshire (Sv1ambo)

The juxtaposition of treasure and trash aptly describes the connection of Dad with the movie *On Her Majesty's Secret Service* (OHMSS). Four Japanese typewriters used as props in one scene in the previously produced James Bond movie *You Only Live Twice* languished in a dark corner. Meanwhile, my Dad had unsuccessfully tried to import Japanese typewriters. Then he somehow found out about the hidden treasures in Pinewood studios. My Dad helped finance OHMSS by paying £100 to purchase these typewriters.

In OHMSS, Tracy Di Vicenzo marries James Bond (007) and drives the Mercury Cougar pictured above to help her husband escape from Irma Bunt and her henchman. In real life, a Secret Service Agent's encounter with criminals is often less dramatic.

I once attended a briefing given by a US Secret Service agent whom I'll call Carol. She opened her address at the

Amherst Chamber of Commerce by excitedly sharing about a recent *controlled drop* in Niagara Falls. Carol explained that she wore a postal carrier's uniform and delivered mail to a criminal as she was covered by nearby agents. As soon as the criminal confirmed his identity, she arrested him. Her face beamed as she told this story.

Carol continued to explain how many people do not realize that in addition to Presidential protection the Secret Service has a mandate to safeguard the US payment and financial systems. Historically, this was accomplished through the enforcement of counterfeiting statutes. Since 1984, the agency's responsibility has been expanded to include the investigation of computer fraud and the criminal preparation of false identification documents.

In 1988, the new crime of Identity Theft was defined to have been committed by anyone who:

> knowingly transfers or uses, without lawful authority, a
> means of identification of another person, with the intent
> to commit, or to aid or abet, an unlawful activity.
> (Identity Theft and Assumption Deterrence Act)

"Has anyone ever been a victim of identity theft?" she asked us. A few hands went up. Then she said unequivocally, "You will all be impacted by this crime, sooner or later." Carol had everyone's attention. She went on to explain that there are several things to keep in mind about securing your identity. When you complete a purchase, you will often have to make some of your personal information available to others. Then, there is always a danger that they might have nefarious intent. To protect our identity, she advised us to take a proactive stance in regards to monitoring the integrity of our data and to keeping our data confidential.

She then told a story about shopping in a department store with her daughter. Carol's vigilant eye was drawn to a lonely stack of completed credit card applications sitting unguarded on a table. She picked them up, held them in the air, walked around the store and asked in a loud voice, "Can I speak to a manager?" Her daughter wanted to hide. Carol encouraged us to develop a suspicious mindset that will make us more aware of ways in which criminal acts might be perpetrated. She continued:

> I am always aware of my surroundings. I keep my credit card in plain sight, so that I don't run the risk of helping someone supplement their income by using a small hand-held scanner to capture and sell my personal information.

> Personally, I will only use an ATM machine that is inside a bank, because the transaction is recorded on video, and it is unlikely that someone has tampered with the machine. If an ATM is in a location that isn't well-monitored, it is possible that a criminal has installed a scanner to capture my card information, and has set up a hidden camera to capture my PIN when I use the ATM to withdraw cash.

Then Carol shifted the focus of her talk to the importance of monitoring the accuracy and integrity of personal information stored by credit bureaus. She recommended that we sign up for three free annual credit reports and then stagger ordering them four months apart. She told us to review checking account and credit card balances regularly – at least weekly. In addition, she encouraged us to use low cost services that notify you whenever an address associated with your Social

Security number is added or changed. She emphasized that this can be a good measure to assure receiving an early alert concerning potential fraud.

To wrap up, Carol talked about the dangers of WiFi. This has made computer access more available, but less secure. She emphasized that the Federal Government uses WiFi, but it is part of the responsibility of the Secret Service to alert agencies to potential data breaches. She has performed inspections using mobile equipment to determine if unintended data or unencrypted information can be scanned from outside government buildings.

Whether it was detecting a potential breach in WiFi security or noticing a stack of applications filled with personal information, Carol always soberly and vigilantly looks for ways to prevent potential criminal acts. She briefed us well on many precautions we should use to reduce the risk of becoming a victim of identity theft.

Despite heeding Carol's warnings, my wife and I recently used a credit card to pay for dinner. Shortly afterwards, we were victims of identity theft. Within minutes, criminals had processed three fraudulent transactions. We were glad that fraud monitoring contained the bank's losses and eliminated personal financial loss.

Just like James Bond, we did what was in our power to escape pursuing criminals. Even then, we still experienced an unavoidable skirmish. Although we now try to be even more cautious when using credit cards, we will doubtlessly need to tackle future incursions.

19. Tackle Low - Tackle Hard - Fearlessly

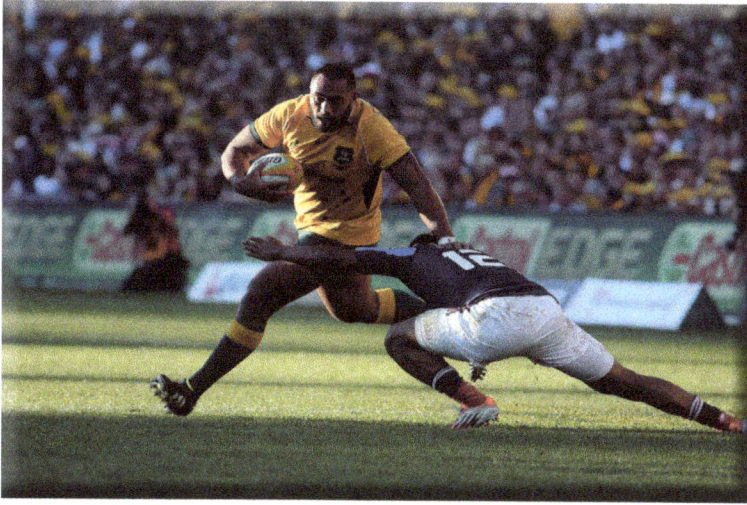

Wallabies vs France – Alliance Stadium, Sydney, Australia
(David Molloy Photography)

Whether in defending my personal identity today or as a teenager playing rugby and protecting the try zone (US Football: End Zone), the same principle increases the likelihood of success, Tackle Low, Tackle Hard, Fearlessly. Who would have ever thought that a lesson learned during intramural sports at Emanuel School in London would have the long-term benefit as a useful technique to apply whenever I am ready to take action.

Whenever I tell Americans that I played rugby for seven years, they usually have the same response, "That's such a dangerous sport. They play without any protection." My experience was that cuts and bruises were the norm, but serious injuries were rare. Only once did I hear of a player who broke his collarbone. Debilitating injuries such as concussions did not plague the sport.

There seems to be an underlying reason why success in rugby is made manifest with less long-term and serious injury. Dr. Warren King believes that the rugby player's mindset is different from that of a US Football player. Dr. King is the Oakland Raider's team physician and has also served the U.S. national rugby team. His observations are insightful:

> I think the biggest thing that football can learn from rugby
> is that, no, you can't use the head as a weapon. Helmets are
> a double edged sword, as they can give an athlete a false
> sense of security. (King)

While a rugby player undoubtedly needs brawn, he also needs his brain to be effective. This was brought home to me at my fortieth high-school reunion when I talked to fellow rugby player, Keith, who was strongly built and well over six feet tall.

Keith asked me, "Do you remember the time when you tackled me and unexpectedly brought me down to the ground?"

I had no recollection of that moment of success. Keith bv recalled a practice when he had shared the best way to tackle. He had said that the key was to have a good technique. If you bring a runner's legs together, this quickly removes the possibility of further forward movement. Then he asked me to demonstrate on him. I gave it my all and surprisingly, he hit the ground with a big thud. I had tackled him low down, quickly and decisively. My unanticipated success was a David and Goliath story. It never occurred to me that it might not work or I might get hurt.

Perhaps our Welsh rugby coach *Taffy Neath* thought the same way, as he helped topple the German Nazis in WW II.

Wilfrid Claude Neath was a retired Flight Lieutenant, who had been awarded a Royal Air Force *Distinguished Flying Cross*. I was told that he was a navigator in bombers from the famous *Dambusters Squadron*. On each bombing raid, the squadron always applied the same methodology. They would fly below the radar just barely above the treetops. It is hard to comprehend the intensity of the experience of providing visual navigational assistance from underneath the fuselage at the nose of the bomber.

The squadron's mission was to destroy infrastructure by striking at the base of the dams with Sir Barnes Wallis's ingeniously designed *Bouncing Bomb*. Shortly before the bomb was dropped, it was given backspin. Because of the low altitude, the bomb fell, hit the water and then moved like a skipping stone. The bomb would not even explode when it first made contact with the dam. Instead the impact would cause a change in the direction of momentum, and this would change the direction of the bomb's spin. The bomb would then hug the dam as gravity caused this explosive charge to sink down deeply into the water and end up close to the dam's base. Then the delayed fuse would detonate the bomb, with great effect.

The *Dambusters* completed a number of wartime missions. The squadron did their part to help Britain tackle and topple Nazi Germany. Their action was yet another tangible demonstration of the wisdom embodied in the principle to tackle an enemy low down, decisively and without being hindered by the paralyzing effects of debilitating fear.

Fear is the emotion that could have risen to the fore when an inspection revealed mold in the basement of the home I wanted to sell. The education I had received by playing rugby first caused me to avoid giving place to fear. Then, I asked myself, "Should I tackle the problem by myself? If so, how should I proceed?" Whenever I face a threat, I first need to find out what options are open to me. This will reveal methodologies that allow me to proceed boldly in what seems to be the best course of action.

Therefore, I first visited the US government's Environmental Protection Agency's website to answer the question, "Is it safe for a homeowner to perform mold remediation themselves?" Because a page provided clear instructions, precautions and techniques, I felt that it would be safe for me embark on this project.

To identify the areas of the basement needing attention and to understand remediation techniques, I hired a mold inspector. With his bright Krypton light, he identified the affected areas and explained safe remediation procedures and techniques.

With the help of a stalwart friend, in about one weekend, the house was readied to pass a home inspection with flying colors. Bold decisive action toppled the mold giant. Fear hadn't deterred me. Help from others had provided a safe course of action.

Many times in life, I have been faced with situations that have unfolded in front of me, and have looked insurmountable. I owe a lot of my success in dealing with these situations to fellow rugby player Keith and to rugby coach *Taffy Neath* who both inspired me to tackle low and hard, and to do so fearlessly.

20. Rome – The Eternal City

Michelangelo's Moses – Church of St. Pietro in Vincoli, Rome (Jackson)

As I was growing up, Rome had a lasting appeal because it was the one place in the world where my parents and I were all relaxed and happy together. We left refreshed by the surroundings.

Rome is known as *The Eternal City* because of its popularization in Hall Caine's 1901 novel of the same name. It is a city that continues to hold special memories for me.

My most vivid memory comes from our first family visit to Rome in the early sixties. We stood on the curb in front of the Colosseum. Five lanes of incessantly fast-moving traffic separated us from this monument. The craziness of the traffic thrilled me even as we all felt our stress levels rise.

The white markings on the road looked like the familiar British Zebra Crossings. In London, the convention was that a driver stopped when they saw that someone wanted to cross the road. This was the signal that it was safe to step off the curb. In Rome, impatient drivers kept on driving without giving thought to our plight.

We observed the locals with horror as they appeared calm when crossing this extremely busy road. With determination, we fearlessly stepped out in front of the oncoming cars and played a game of chicken. Drivers weaved around us. Because we were in Rome, we had to do as the Romans do. We walked at a steady pace, but also kept one eye open – just in case. Later, I would quip, "If a driver hits you on the crossing, it's their fault." Some consolation.

After years of my parents' sacrifice and hardship, the family's Japanese to English translation business had reached the point where we could afford to take an annual three-week European trip. We travelled by train, spending most of the time roaming around Italy. We generally stayed in Rome at the beginning and ending of each trip. As a family, we visited Italy about seven times. Over the decades, I have personally stayed in Rome for about six months of my life. I love the City. It has been a source of endless joy, a place where I have gone to regain perspective at critical junctures of my life.

When my parents made the trips, my Dad had to plan carefully because, in England, the Exchange Control Act restricted the amount of foreign currency we could take out of the country. In 1966, Britain restricted individual foreign currency purchases for personal travel to £50 (Peel). Based on historical exchange rates this was only $163 (Todd).

Because we had to travel frugally, my Dad devoured each new edition of the must have book, *Europe on $5 per day*, which debuted a few years earlier in 1957. Recently, Arthur Frommer reminisced about his experiences while writing his early editions:

> I found a three course dinner for the equivalent of 90 U.S. cents at a Left Bank restaurant in Paris and a hotel in Florence fronting the Arno River, where sunny and spacious rooms came for $3 a night. (Frommer)

As a family, we had learned to live modestly. We found affordable *Pensiones* (Small hotels), cafes that served coffee and grocery shops. We smuggled food into our hotel rooms. I explored the streets and sights of Rome. Mum and Dad treated themselves to ice-chip covered watermelon from street vendors. We all had fun.

To conserve foreign currency, Dad would use pounds sterling to purchase railways passes in England. These passes provided unlimited travel on Italian trains. On one occasion during a train ride from Mafia controlled Sicily, a Roman befriended us and invited me to stay with his family. It was a fantastic three weeks.

Crazy as Rome is, it was always a home away from home for my parents. Like homing pigeons, we kept returning.

A few years ago, I was trying to figure out the draw that Rome clearly had on our family and subsequently on my own life. I came up with several logical reasons, but then a revelation provided me with a profound insight.

Periodically, I find that the stress of life brings me to the point that I lose perspective. A trip to Rome always restores my equilibrium. Although founded in 753 BC (Roman Republic), the city still survives. The Roman Empire has come and it has gone, but the city still stands. This is a tangible reminder that people are resilient even if not all structures will withstand the test of time.

I grew up wandering through the streets of London, looking at buildings, visiting museums and enjoying watching the hustle and bustle which city life brings. I like to wander in large cities. Because Rome is very compact, in about fifty minutes you can walk from the southeast corner where the Colosseum is located to the Vatican in the northwest corner of this ancient city. Rome is the perfect size in which to take the walks that I love. I can engage in a healthy interesting pursuit and also be afforded plenty of time to think and reflect.

Mum and Dad enjoyed Italy because it brought back pleasant memories from the past. They felt estranged in England, but in Italy they felt warmly embraced. I realized that Rome was the only place in the world where I consistently saw them at peace.

My parents needed a place in which to be nurtured and to be restored. The eternal city of Rome welcomed them. Following my parents' lead, I still continue to answer Rome's call for me to return. They had stumbled upon a key to survival. Mum and Dad found a place of refuge and renewal to which they returned year after year.

21. Stand by Me

Mum & Dad – *Letchworth State Park NY* (Lambert, Private Collection)

My parents found peace in Rome. Before that they had travelled the world: Neath (Wales), Kyushu (Japan), London, Tokyo, Hong Kong, London and finally Gillingham (Medway Towns, Kent). The picture above reminds me that they bravely overcame many challenges together. They embraced and lived by the words in these lyrics:

> When the night has come
> And the land is dark
> And the moon is the only light we'll see
> No I won't be afraid
> Oh, I won't be afraid
> Just as long as you stand, stand by me
> (Leiber, Stoller & King)

The picture on the previous page was taken in 1984, shortly before my parents attended my wedding in Williamsville, NY. My Mum and Dad sat right behind me. During most of the ceremony, I could hear my Dad crying. My Mum responded, "Don't be so silly." This was the only time I can ever remember when my Dad expressed such intense emotion. His upbringing in a Japanese family of Samurai descent made it extremely difficult for him to show emotion in ways that are more common in the West, such hugging, or saying, "I love you." He demonstrated his deep love and commitment to our family welfare through relentlessly performing acts of service.

My Mum grew up in Neath. Her Dad was a Methodist Minister, who ran his Christian library and bookshop in the center of town. Around the turn of the century, he would ride his bicycle up and down the Rhonda Valley, preaching the Gospel to the coal miners. He was an active participant in the Welsh Revival. Mum was artistic and musical, and dreamed of becoming an architect. At that time, women did not become architects.

Mum did various jobs, and was a primary school teacher in Horsham (Surrey). One day she told me, "My sisters were getting married. I didn't want to be left on the shelf. She continued with her Welsh lilt, I didn't really love my first husband, you know. He was a bit of a pervert."

The Second World War broke out. The inspired oratory of Winston Churchill reignited the embers of optimism in my parents who lived on opposite sides of the globe and did not yet know each other. My Mum's friends in London and my Dad's Foreign Office colleagues in Shanghai (China), Singapore

(Malaysia) and New Delhi (India) provided them with the encouragement they needed to survive the war.

After the war had ended, they met on one fateful day at 57 Camden Square in London.

My Mum attended a party at which my Dad was present. It was love at first sight. She later said:

> My heart went pita pat. However, I was already married. I fought the idea of marrying someone from Japan. After all, so many atrocities had been committed by the Japanese military. How could I possibly get a divorce and marry him? What would my Father say?

Irrational love prevailed. Despite my Grandfather's stony response, they married. After a few years of marriage, they decided to start a new life in Tokyo, where I was born. They lived in occupied Japan and together they were again integrated back into society. My Mum told me that Baron Harada, the head of the Imperial Household, invited my parents to visit the Palace. Sadly, the occupying allied forces denied permission for Dad and Mum to accept the invitation. Then student riots erupted in Japan, and my Mum felt nervous as a westerner in a foreign land. They decided that it was time to flee Japan with a six-month old child, me. We ended up in a refugee camp in Hong Kong until the Salvation Army helped repatriate us back to England.

There was no welcome mat on our return. Society could not wrap its head around the justification for a British lady to divorce an English gentleman and to marry a man who in the minds of most was the embodiment of a defeated and hated enemy. In contrast, my Mum's brother-in-law Eric, who had worked in intelligence during World War II, understood the critical importance of my Dad's contribution and spoke highly of him. My Dad was a man of few words, but once said of Eric, "He is a very kind man."

Most of society viewed their mixed marriage as taboo and provided few words of encouragement. As an antidote, my Mum and Dad nurtured their growing love and affection for each other and for me. Their dialog with each other was the catalyst that enabled them to garner a sufficient level of optimism needed to finish their races strongly. They fled many times. They fought many battles. They fought for each other. They fought for me.

I had a ringside view of the many battles, which my parents faced together. There was a tenant who attacked my Mum. At the time of the trial, I was sent away to be cared for in Littlehampton, Sussex Mr. Bunting, a holder of a private mortgage attempted to claim that my parents had defaulted on their payments. Another tenant attempted to bring charges against my Dad for harassment. If you knew my Dad, you would never believe that he was capable of harassing anyone.

Repeatedly, their mutual encouragement allowed them to soldier on and to avoid being vanquished. Even in difficult situations they were still able to see a glimmer of hope.

Mum and Dad were living examples of the truth that opposites attract. They demonstrated fidelity and faithfulness to each other. I am grateful that they fully embraced Winston Churchill's admonition to never give in. I am the person I am today because they always stood by each other and by me.

References

Adams, A. (1943). Winter storm, Manzanar Relocation Center, California. Retrieved from loc.gov

Allen, W. (1977). *Yale University Press Book of Quotations*. Retrieved from books.google.com

Associated Press. (2005, September 22). *Emergency landing televised on JetBlue flight*. Retrieved from nbcnews.com

Audio Fair Supplement. (1963). *Tape Recording Magazine*, 1963(5). Retrieved from americanradiohistory.com

Barker, G. (Circa 1883). *Niagara Falls Ice Bridge*. Photograph. US Library of Congress, Washington DC.

Bialik, C. (2010, September 4). *Seven Careers in a Lifetime? Think Twice, Researchers Say*. Retrieved from wsj.com

Cambridge University Press. (2015). *British English Dictionary & Thesaurus*. Retrieved from dictionary.cambridge.org.

Carrigan, D. (1938). *The meaning and origin of the expression: Fly by the seat of one's pants*. Retrieved from phrases.org.uk

Churchill, W. (1940, June 6). *We Shall Fight on the Beaches*. Retrieved from winstonchurchill.org

Churchill, W. (1941, October 29). *Never Give In*. Retrieved from winstonchurchill.org

Clinton, H. (1996). *It Takes a Village*. Simon & Shuster. New York.

David Molloy Photography. (2014, June 21). *Wallabies vs France*. Retrieved from flickr.com

Detroit Publishing Company. (Circa 1890 to 1900). *Piccadilly Circus, London, England*. Print. US Library of Congress, Washington DC.

Efekt. (2008, July 26). *Tetsworth Car Boot Sale*. Retrieved from flickr.com

Frommer. (2013, November 15). *Europe on $5 a day? You must be joking!* Retrieved from dailymail.co.uk

Hirkimer, Sir. (1960). *Wide Open*. Retrieved from flickr.com

Hirkimer, Sir. (1963). *Stewarts Lane*. Retrieved from flickr.com

Hradecky, S. (2008, November 29). *JetBlue A320 at Los Angeles on Sep 21st 2005*. Retrieved from avherald.com

Identity Theft and Assumption Deterrence Act Amendment. (1998, October 30). Public Law 105-318, 112 Stat. 3007. Retrieved from ftc.gov

International News. (1940, December). *London is still "taking it"*. Photograph. US Library of Congress, Washington DC.

King, W. (2013, October 15). *Concussions: Rugby Can Help Football*. Retrieved from the postgame.com

Knowles, E. (2005). *Oxford dictionary of phrase and fable* (2nd ed.). Oxford: Oxford University Press.

Lane, L. (2015, March 27). *High Anxiety: Comparative Stats on Flying, Health, and Safety in The Wake of a Plane Crash*. Retrieved from forbes.com

Leiber, Stoller, King. (1960). *Ben E. King Lyrics - Stand by Me.* Retrieved from azlyrics.com

Lennon, J. (1967). *All You Need is Love.* Retrieved from metrolyrics.com

Leovy, J. (2005, September 22). *For Passengers, Humor, Tears -- Then Cheers.* Retrieved from latimes.com

Lerner, A. (1964). *My Fair Lady "Wouldn't it be Loverly" Lyrics.* Retrieved from reelclassics.com

Mason, S. (1914). *Bibliography of Oscar Wilde.* London: T.W. Laurie.

Mc Hough, P. (2013). Chapter 1. In *STABS: Raw Recruits* (pp.2-22). London: Publish Nation.

McFerrin. (1988). *Don't Worry, Be Happy.* Retrieved from artists.letssingit.com

McGowan, J.E. (2014, June 29). *Cricket Action.* Retrieved from flickr.com.

National Weather Service. (1977). *An Overview of the Blizzard.* Retrieved from noaa.gov

Palmer, Alfred. (1942, October) *Production. C-47 Transport Planes.* Photograph. US Library of Congress, Washington DC.

Peel, J. *Hansard Report.* (1969, June 30). House of Commons Debate 786. Retrieved from hansard.millbankssystems.com

Reuters. (1965, January 27). *UK: Sir Winston Churchill Lies in State in Westminster Hall.* Retrieved from itnsource.com

Robinson, K., & Aronica, L. (2009). Chapter 1. *The element: How finding your passion changes everything.* (pp.1-26). New York: Viking.

Roman Republic (2014, November 20). In *Encyclopaedia Britannica.* Retrieved from Britannica.com

Russell, Lee. (1942). *Swimming Lesson.* Rupert, Idaho. Photograph. US Library of Congress, Washington DC.

Shakespeare, W. (n.d.). *As you like it.* Retrieved from goodreads.com

Shakespeare, W. (n.d.). *Othello.* Retrieved from goodreads.com

Simon, Paul. (1965, June 23). *I Am A Rock.* Retrieved from paulsimon.com

Stevensen. (2007, September 9). *Bodies in Motion.* Retrieved from flickr.com

Sv1ambo. (2011, June 8). *1969 Mercury Cougar XR7 CJ428 Convertible – James Bond.* Retrieved from flickr.com

Todd, Michael. (2007, January 10). *Historical Dollar Exchange Rates.* Retrieved from miketodd.net

Utamaro, Kitagawa. (Between 1801 and 1804). *Sake zuki.* Print. US Library of Congress, Washington DC.

Vinocur, Jeffrey M. (2006). *University of Pennsylvania LOVE Sculpture.* Retrieved from commons.wikimedia.org

Warner, G. (2014, January 7). *As bad as the Blizzard of '77? No way - The Buffalo News.* Retrieved from buffalonews.com

Wholey, Dennis. (1998). Serenity. In *The miracle of change: The path to self-discovery and spiritual* growth (p. 242). New York: Pocket Books.

Woodhouse, J. (2007). *Strategies for healthcare education: How to teach in the 21st century.* Oxford: Radcliffe Publishing

Index

1960's Music. 19, 49, 62, 81
1980's Music. 62
1986. 67
2010. 45
9-11 Attack 4, 40

ACoA (Adult Children of Alcoholics) . 18
Air Canada 38
Airbus 37-38
Airport 22, 38
Albany (NY) 62
Alcoholism 18
All I Want is a Room Somewhere 6
All the World's a Stage. 45
All you Need is Love 49
Allen, Woody 53
Alliance Stadium (Sydney) 73
Alps 40, 64, 66
Amherst (NY) 70
Anglican Church 66
Aquaphobia 29
Arding & Hobbs (London) 66
As You Like it. 45
Association for Information
Management (ASLIB) 8
Associated Press 38
ATM crimes 71
Australia. 73

Baby It's Cold Outside 25-28
Battersea (London). 5-8,18
BBC World Service 15
Beanie Babies 67
Beatles 49, 59
Beaulieu (Hampshire) 69
Beaumont Plateau (PA) 53
Berkley (CA) 38
Blackie – No. 45154 (London). 61
Blitz, WWII (London) 9-10
Blizzard of '77 (Buffalo, NY) 25-26
Bolton Abbey (Skipton) 57
Bomb, Bouncing 75
Bombing, Buzz, Incendiary &
Terrorist 9-12
Bond, James (007) 69
Boot Sale. 65
Bound Brook (NJ). 22-23
British Airways 21
British Broadcasting Corp. (BBC) . . 15

British Citizenship 15
British Foreign Office. 14, 16, 82
British Standards Institution (BSI). . . 8
Buffalo (NY) 25-28, 39, 46, 62, 63
Bush House (London) 15

C-47 Transport Plane. 37
Caine, Hall. 77
Calais (France) 29
California 13, 37
Camden Square (London). 83
Canada. 38
Central Atlantic Collegiate
Conference Championships (CACC) 53
Championship Watches 56
Charity. 66-67
Chatham (Kent) 23
Chemical Engineering 58
Chemical Plant Design. 58
Chernobyl Nuclear Plant. 67
China. 16, 82
Christian Library (Neath, Wales) . . . 82
Christian Missionary School (Japan) . 8
Churchill, Sir Winston . . 8, 9-12, 82, 84
Clapham Junction (London) 66
Clinton, Hilary 49
Coal 61, 82
Colosseum (Rome) 77-78, 80
Commercial Rental Property 41
Community Hospital (Nyack NY) . . 46
Computer Applications 58
Computer Consultancy 60
Concussions. 73
Cork 30
Cornwall (England) 26
Courtaulds Manufacturing 58
Cricket 41
Crimes 33
Cross Country Championships . . 53-56

Dambusters Squadron 75
David and Goliath 74
Decca Radio and TV (Battersea) 5
Devon (England). 26, 41
Diana, Princess 18
Diesel Engine 62
Discrimination 7
Distinguished Flying Cross 75
Dogs Home (Battersea) 5

Dominican Republic . . . 49, 50, 51, 53
Don't Worry be Happy 62
Doolittle, Eliza 6
Dover (Kent) 29

Elephant & Castle (London) 35
Emanuel School (London) 18, 73
Emergency Landings 37-39
Emergency Room 47
Entrepreneur 60
Environmental Protection Agency
 (EPA). 76
Erie County (NY) 42, 44
Eternal City 77-80
Europe 8, 77-80
Euston Station (London) 11
Exchange Control Act 78

Fairmount Park, Philadelphia (PA) 53-56
Fear of Drowning 32
Fear of Dying 27
Ferries, Channel 30
Fight on the beaches 10
Fire 9
Floatation 30
Florida 26
Football 74
Foreclosure 41
Foreign Currency Control 79
Foreign Office (London) . . . 14, 15-16, 82
France 24, 30
French National Rugby 73
Frommer, Arthur 79
Functioning Alcoholic 18

Gamages Department Store 67
Garage Sale (Boot Sale) 65
Gillingham (Kent) 23, 66, 81
Google 66
Gower Street (London) 8
Gulf Stream 26

H-1B Visa 59
Habitat for Humanity 68
Hall of Kings (Westminster) 12
Hampshire (England) 69
Harada, Baron (Tokyo, Japan) 83
Harrods Department Store 11
Hayes Wharf (London) 7
Heart Failure 47
Heathrow Airport (London) 21
Hitler 9, 40
HK Lewis 8

HM Customs and Excise 7
HM Factory Inspectorate 3
Holborn (London) 66
Holidays 64
Holocaust 6
Hong Kong Refugee Camp . . . 81, 83
Horsham (Surrey) 82
House Among the Roses 45-46
Household Calvary 11
Houses of Parliament (London) . . . 11
Housing Tribunal (London) 6
Hyde Park (London) 11

I am a rock; I am an island 19
Ian Allen Publications 61
Ice Bridge (Niagara Falls, NY) 25
Idaho 29
Identity Theft 70-72
Imperial College of Science,
 Technology & Medicine
 (Kensington, London) . . . 11, 18, 21, 58
Imperial Household (Japan) 83
Independent Television News 12
India 83
Industrial Safety 2-3
Inland Revenue 58
Internment Camps, Japanese . . . 13-16
Interstate Highways 63
Irish Republican Army (IRA) 9, 11
Italy 77-80
ITN (Independent Television News) . . 12

Jackson, Anne Elisabeth 45-48, 54
Japan 13, 15, 18, 81, 83
Japanese American National
 Museum 14
Japanese Military 13, 83
Japanese Translation Business
 . . . . 7, 18, 78
JetBlue 37-38
JFK Airport 22
Jumbo Jet 38

Kensington Palace (London) . . . 18, 58
Kent (England) 30, 66, 81
Kentish Town Station
 (Camden, London) 61
Kew Gardens (London) 15
Kings Cross Station (London) 11
Kyushu (Japan) 15, 81

Lancaster (NY) 48
Landing Gear 37

Latchmere (London). 29
Left Bank (Paris) 79
Leicester Square. 6
Lenon, John 49
Lerner 6
Letchworth State Park (NY) 81
Library 8, 82
Linde Industrial Gas Division . . . 22
Lines Brothers. 66
Littlehampton (Sussex) 84
Lockerbie (Scotland). 40
London, City of (England) 9
London (England) 5-12, 20, 23, 33-6, 81-4
Long Beach (CA) 37
Los Angeles (CA) 13, 38
LP Records (33's) 35
Lying in State (Westminster) 12
Lynmouth (Devon) 41

Mafia. 79
Malaysia. 83
Manzanar Relocation Center (CA). . 13
Mara, Commissioner Dan 54
Marathon 56
Marine Expeditionary Unit (MEU) . . 1
Marriage, Mixed 84
Mason-Dixon Line 68
Martin, Lonnie (USMC). 1
Medway Towns (England) 81
Mercury Cougar 69
Methodist Minister 82
Michelangelo 77
Michigan. 31
Minic Motorways. 66
Mission. 50, 67
Mixed Marriage. 84
Model Railway (00 Gauge) 66
Mold Remediation 75
Monet, Claude 46
Moses Sculpture (Michelangelo) . . . 77
Music. 6, 19, 45
My Fair Lady. 6

National Archives (College Park, MD) 15
National Archives (Kew Gardens) . . 15
National Museum of USMC
   (Triangle, VA) 1
National Park Service 31
National Weather Service
   (Buffalo, NY). 25
Navigator, Flight 75
Nazi Germany 10, 75
NCAA 53-56

Neath (Wales) 81, 82
Neath, Wilfrid Claude (Flight
   Lieutenant, DFC) 74-75
Never Give in 8, 84
Newark Airport. 22
Newfoundland (Canada) 26
New Delhi (India). 83
New Jersey 22
New York (NY) 22, 38, 40
New York State . . . 31, 42, 60, 61, 81
New York State Thruway 62
New York State Troopers 46
NFL (Oakland Raiders). 74
Niagara Falls (NY) 25, 70
Nine Elms (London). 7
North Atlantic Drift. 26
Not-for-Profit (Charity) 66
Nuclear Plant Disaster 67
Nyack College (Nyack, NY). . . . 46, 54

Oakland Raiders (CA) 74
Occupational Safety & Health
   Administration (OSHA) 3
On Her Majesty's Secret Service. . . . 69
Othello 33
Oxfordshire (England) 65

Palace of Westminster Staff
   (London). 12
Palm Trees. 26
Pan Am Flight 103
   (Lockerbie, Scotland) 40
Paris (France). 79
Patent Office (UK) 58
Pennsylvania 49, 53
PhD. 18, 23, 47, 58
Philadelphia (PA) 49, 53-57
Physician 46, 74
Physics. 30
Piccadilly Circus (London) 33
Pinewood Studios
   (Iver Heath, Buckinghamshire) . . . 69
Piracy 1
Popular Music. 19, 49, 62, 81
Post University Eagles
   Men's Cross Country Team 56
Power Station (Battersea) 5
Prayer 37
Propaganda, Radio 15
Property Taxes 42
Public Swimming Pool. 29
Puerto Rico 50
Purse. 33

Radio Broadcasting Propaganda . . .15
Railway Children 67
Railway Tracks 61
Raintree Island Apartments (NY) . . 31
Refugee Camp (Hong Kong) 83
Rent Control Tribunal 6
Rhonda Valley (Wales) 82
Richmond (VA) 28, 63
Robbery 33
Roman Empire 80
Rome (Italy) 8, 40, 77-80, 81
Royal Air Force (RAF) 58, 75
Royal Household 12
Rugby 73-76
Rupert (ID) 29
Russia 67

Sake Wine 17
Salvation Army 83
Samurai 15, 16, 82
Sargent Major Martin 1
Scotland 40
Scotland Yard's Special Branch . . . 16
Second World War 9-10, 20, 75
Secret Service (US) 70
Shakespeare, William 33, 45
Shanghai (China) 16, 82
Sicily (Italy) 79
Simon, Paul 19
Singapore (Malaysia) 15, 82
Skipton (North Yorkshire) 57
Sleeping Bear Dunes 31
Smoking 17
Snow Storm 25-26, 62
Social Security Number 71
Soviet Union (USSR) 67
St Paul's Cathedral (London) 9
St. Pietro in Vincoli (Rome) 77
Stand by Me 81
Starr, Ringo 59
Steam Train 5, 61
Stewarts Lane (Battersea) 5
Sticky Wicket 41
Strutton Ground (London) 7
Swimming Lessons 29-32
Switzerland 64
Sydney (Australia) 73
Syracuse (NY) 62

Taffy Neath 75
Terrorism 11, 40
Theft 33
Tetsworth (Oxfordshire) 65

Tokyo (Japan) 81, 83
Tokyo Rose 15
Tonawanda (NY) 20, 22, 31
Toronto Pierson Airport (Canada) . . 38
Torquay (Devon) 26
Train Spotter 61
Trains 61-62, 79
Tri-ang Model Railways 66
Triangle (VA) 1
TY Inc 67

United Kingdom 43
Ukraine 67
Unilever 58
Union Carbide 20, 21-24, 59
University of Pennsylvania 49
US Embassy (London) 7
US Marine Corps (USMC) 1, 4
US National Rugby Team 74
US Postal Service carrier 69
US Secret Service 69
USSR 67

Vacations 64
Vatican (Rome) 80
Victoria Station (London) 7, 11
Vinyl Records 35
Virginia 60, 63

Wales (United Kingdom) 81
Wallabies Ruby Team 73
Wallis, Sir Barnes 75
Wartime Radio Propaganda 15
Washington Beltway (DC) 63
We Shall Fight on the Beaches 10
Welsh Revival 82
Westminster Hall (London) 12
Wholey, Dennis 17
WiFi Security 72
Williamsville (NY) 82
Wilson, Prime Minister Harold . . . 12
Wing, Aircraft 37
Winnie 9
Woolworths 34
World War II (WW II)
. . . . . . 9-10, 13-16, 20, 37, 75, 82, 83
World Trade Towers (NY) 40

Yorkshire, North (England) 57
You Only Live Twice   69

Zebra Crossing 78

www.ingramcontent.com/pod-product-compliance
Lightning Source LLC
Chambersburg PA
CBHW041301040426
42334CB00028BA/3109